A Garden of
Miracles

A Garden of Miracles

Herbal drinks for pleasure, health and beauty

JILL DAVIES

With a foreword by
Kitty Campion

Beaufort Books
Publishers
New York

First American edition

Published in the United States by Beaufort Books Publishers, New York.

First published in Great Britain in 1985 by Frederick Muller.

Frederick Muller is an imprint of Muller, Blond & White Limited, 55/57 Great Ormond Street, London, WC1N 3HZ.

Illustrations copyright ©1985 Muller, Blond & White Limited
Illustrations by Rodney Paull

Library of Congress Cataloging in Publication Data

Davies, Jill.
    A garden of miracles.

    1. Herbs – Therapeutic use.   2. Herbal teas.
3. Herbs.   4. Herb gardening.   I. Title.
RM666.H33D38 1985   615'.321   84–24413
ISBN   0–8253–0285–4
ISBN   0–8253–0286–2 (pbk.)
10 9 8 7 6 5 4 3 2 1

Printed and bound in Great Britain by R.J. Acford, Chichester, Sussex

Contents

Dedicated to Nick for his loving and giving
also to our children and family for all the joy they bring us

Foreword

The first time I met Jill she paid me a wonderful compliment: she assured me a book I'd recently written was the best of its kind. Now I'm in a position to reciprocate and the compliment comes from the head as well as the heart. This really is the best book ever written on the art of making herbal drinks and on their myriad uses. The instructions are clear and simple and will guide and inspire anyone who has never even tried a cup of herbal tea. Each herb used is clearly identified and described and the reasons why certain herbs are blended together is given, together with their actions on the body. So amateurs need not feel intimidated. This book also contains a wealth of information for those who are familiar with herbal teas but may be feeling a bit jaded about the predictable taste of a single herb, and it encourages a sense of adventure sensibly moderated with discrimination.

As a medical herbalist I used to treat my daily herbal teas as a penance rather than a pleasure. I had long understood the reasons why I shouldn't be drinking conventional tea or coffee but despaired of ever finding anything enjoyable to drink in their place. Then Jill showed me how good even the most dire medicinal teas can be made to taste. Her idea of orchestrating flavours by adding essential oils to dried herbs is revolutionary and when she marries this with her wide understanding of the subtle alchemy of herbs her resulting teas are a treat for the taste buds. What is even more important is that they're positively beneficial for the health in contrast to tea and coffee which are actively detrimental . . . which goes to prove that not all life's pleasures are illegal, immoral or fattening.

Kitty Campion

Shropshire 1984

Acknowledgments

I want to thank so many people who helped make this book possible and perhaps top of the list comes the publishers, but a close second is my family for their help and support. Thank you to Nick particularly for the brilliant inspiration for the book title. And to my father Mr David Davies who found the intriguing tea excerpt about my relation. Thank you, too, to Dr Christopher and The School of Natural Healing who gave me confidence and much more.

A large thank you goes to Dr G. W. Pike for our partnership and help in the commercial development of the tea-bag range. Thanks also to The British Herb Trade Association whose continual support is welcome. Thank you Barbara Griggs for being so generous with her own resources and always remembering our teas. I must also thank Cambridge Botanic Gardens and especially Mr King who gladly and willingly opened up their wonderful library so we could use the beautiful plant pictures in this book. And, most importantly, a very large and warm thank you to my friend and excellent typist Sue Strickland, whose spelling, speed and general ability to decipher dreadful handwriting turned this book into a reality.

Last, but by no means least, many thanks to all the visitors, letter writers, 'phone callers and patients who helped make this book happen.

chapter one

Why herbal drinks?

The drinking or imbibing of any liquid serves many functions: to quench thirst, for ritual, comfort and sharing, to produce a state of altered consciousness, and to warm, cool and feed. Nowadays, the accepted punctuation to the day is the drinking of the 'herbs' tea and coffee. Their stimulating effects have made them universally popular, but there are many good reasons to cut out excessive drinking of these two favourites . . .

Coffee: its chemistry, uses and abuses

In the Sudan and in Abyssinia, where the coffee plant grows wild, the natives chew the berry raw, as a stimulant. They know the limitations of this plant and know that, occasionally and in its raw, whole state, it is useful. (All poisonous plants are useful at certain times and coffee's stimulative qualities can halt comatose or reverse other poisons.) However, moderate and certainly excessive intake by anybody may cause insomnia, muscle tremor, restlessness and overworking of the kidneys and the bowel – the latter, in turn, causing constipation. Excessive caffeine consumption can contribute to agoraphobia due to continual autonomic overactivity, giving way to a lower than normal threshold of panic. High caffeine consumption may, in addition, contribute to the precipitation of acute hypoglycaemia due to worn out adrenals. (Coffee strips the adrenal glands of two B vitamins, choleine and inositol, and this, in turn, lowers the body's resistance to infection, increases demineralisation of the bones, and water retention can occur. It can also cause the constant robbing of proteins, and may eat away our stomach cells and give us ulcers.) Caffeine toxicity can even produce cognitive impairment (delirium). Most dangerous of all, it can cause heart palpitations and tachycardia.

A recent story told to me by a fellow herbal practitioner illustrates the general public's short memory concerning the harmful effects of coffee. A woman, who was, in fact, working at an NHS hospital at the time, found herself getting quite drastic heart palpitations and feared the worst. Several tests were carried out and a thorough case history was taken by the staff. No clues or answers were thrown up by these efforts and her condition deteriorated to the point that she feared severe heart attacks. Her fear increased one day while she hung around to hear the results of yet further and more complicated tests. As she waited, a friend (the herbal practitioner) turned up to keep her company as she had just heard of her problem and sought to provide moral support.

During the course of an hour, my friend counted the number of cups of coffee she consumed – something in the region of five cups from a dispensing machine. She then pronounced her diagnosis about her friend's heart problem: simply too much coffee. Not surprisingly, the advice fell on deaf ears at first from the staff involved in the testing so far. However, her powers of persuasion to cut out coffee for a period resulted in a clean bill of health after a very short time, with a complete elimination of any recurrent heart palpitations. Not least was the saving of the cost of an operation to the N.H.S., who pronounced this to be the next step if the tests proved inconclusive.

What is looked upon as normal consumption of coffee per day, i.e. five cups, can cause some or all of the previously catalogued symptoms within a very short period of time. A host of allergies and problems are often relieved by simply leaving coffee out of a diet – for instance, migraine, eczema, arthritis, and more. The constituents of coffee give clues to its potential dangers and the reasons that it has been and still is occasionally used in medicine – and should, therefore, be consumed with care.

The berries (and, more so, the leaves) of coffee (*coffea arabica*) contain caffeine (1–2 per cent) and this is almost identical to theine, the active principle of tea (also found in beef). Its action is stimulating to the intellectual powers and induces sleeplessness, hence its great value in narcotic poisoning – in acute cases it can be injected into the rectum by enema. This is sometimes done to people with a highly toxic illness, cancer being one. It is also useful in cases of snake bites where a coma is inevitable if not intercepted. As caffeine increases the force of the heart it can be useful in medicine if used in conjunction with digitalis.

Coffee's other constituents are volatile oils, colouring matter, tannin, traces of theobromine and theophylline, gum, sugar and protein.

Tea: its chemistry, uses and abuses

Interestingly enough, tea is not used medicinally in this country, though it has been in the past, for the relief of neuralgic headaches. It contains, however, twice the amounts of caffeine (2–4 per cent) as coffee, and it would seem that coffee got its bogus name of caffeine poisoner mainly because most people made very strong cups of coffee, thus imbibing more caffeine per cup than tea.

The theine in tea, like caffeine, makes it a very strong stimulant, exciting the nervous system and producing a state of exhilaration and comfort. In poor countries, where the leaves are harvested, they are eaten green, even stronger in stimulative action and vital for the people to carry out their hard work with often little to eat. It also has an astringent action due to its tannin content (which curbs feelings of hunger). Perhaps this is the reason many people drink tea with evening supper. However, tannin in large quantities (especially near meal times or with meals) has a negative effect on true protein digestibility. Tannin concentration is also present in coffee, it must not be forgotten: both can be labelled anti-nutritional, while both, but largely tea, also inhibit iron absorption. All this can produce indigestion and low energy levels, with 'black tea' appearing to be the worst offender.

Tea's other constituents are gallotannic acid, boheic acid, volatile oils, aquerus extract, protein wax, resin, ash and theophylline. This string of chemical constituents is held in high esteem in China, where the action of tea upon the system is never considered by the Chinese to be anything but beneficial.

In some other countries, their tea is drunk green (particularly favouring the wild species collected on the hillsides), being rapidly dried and fired while being drunk as an infusion. In this country, we 'brew' our tea, steeping a lot of leaves for a long time – also we tend to use Indian tea. In India, the same tea goes through an additional process, that of fermentation, before firing, producing a 'black tea'. Although these black and green teas can be made from the same tea plant species, Indian species do make a better black tea and Chinese ones a better green one. However, this black tea does not have the same beneficial merits as the green variety.

The preparation of the green China tea is exactly the same as for herbal tea in this country, while its properties are known to the Chinese to be of general medicinal use, regulating body temperature, removing flatulence, invigorating the constitution and promoting digestion. There are many hundreds of different tea species and all are used in various medicinal ways – to make up an eye wash, to provide a nourishing broth, to check dysentery or to act as an anti-haemorrhagic. Furthermore, the Chinese brews do not possess the deleterious substances found in the imported varieties, including salts of copper, to name but one impurity, which largely help to cause tea's bad effects and numb any good ones.

De-caffeination?
Just a mention here about the wave of interest in drinking de-caffeinated

3

coffee. This de-caffeination removes only part of the harm of coffee's complex and natural chemistry and, in fact, it is the acids that are left behind which are just as dangerous, if not more so. A good coffee substitute would be a dandelion or chicory roast. While the better teas to drink are those containing less acids and tannins, which are the China teas rather than the Indian varieties. China teas are also generally drunk without milk, which also ensures that they are made far weaker.

Herbal alternatives

Of course there are millions of plants on this planet of which coffee and tea plants are but two. Many are very powerful and extremely dangerous; many have unpleasant flavours, whereas some are very pleasant; some are highly medicinal, some poisonous. National drinks, cultural tastes, customs and fashions all dictate what one drinks, wherever one lives. But, like anything, habits slowly change and one change is the acceptance of herbal teas or tisanes. This is because people are rebelling against the side effects of drugs in general – and tea and coffee come under that heading.

The beauty of herbal teas

There is a herbal drink to suit almost every mood, emotion and physical need for all times of the day: taking forty winks, enjoying a good sleep, calming and refreshing, invigorating, nausea subduing and stimulating. All these attributes of herbal teas are well known by most other European countries, where the drinking of herbal teas in some families is part of an old tradition. For instance, in Austria (where, incidentally, the coffee house is supreme), children tend to be brought up on herb teas, not being given tea or coffee until they become young adults. The same could be said of Belgium, France and Switzerland. In general, the drinking of herbal teas is popular while herbalist shops survive and some knowledge of herbs is kept alive in most families. My own part-Belgian mother-in-law knew the benefits of chamomile long before I did.

Another great advantage of herbal teas is that they can be drunk singly or blended carefully with six or ten ingredients to produce the required effect. Just as many different types of tea leaf go to make one brand label, so many varieties of chamomile and its essential oil can make a very special chamomile tea. In addition, instead of leaving the mixing and blending to established firms and factories to make the flavour choices for our tea and coffee, herb teas can be mixed and blended at home to suit one's own purposes. Certainly this is what early man did, although early man had many more instincts intact and a natural knowledge of the flora around him because he was continually in close harmony with himself and his surroundings, as his ancestors had been. So nowadays much more caution and learning application must be applied. In the past, at least one member of the family was familiar with the uses of herbs. Now at least one member of the family is probably familiar with a calculator or more complicated computer. What we must do is marry the two.

The medicinal powers of herb teas

In China, herbal teas are not only a way of life, they are firmly part of traditional medicine. Traditional medicine works hand in hand with western medicine (as they call it) at the harmonious instructions of the Communist regime. Herbal teas provide cures for a range of illnesses and are cheap and easy to prescribe, mostly because the recipient has to make his or her own brew from virtually unprocessed plants. These herbs – chrysanthemum root, magnolia root and other indigenous plants – are collected wild from the hillsides in country districts and their main role is to provide preventative medicine for the children and adults of each community. Unceremoniously brewed in a huge cauldron, the tea is poured into a bucket and every morning slopped into the mug of each person. The bloodstream is cleaned, toxins removed, the system balanced and health generally maintained for very little money. And the taste? Rather pleasant.

In the Chinatowns of Canada and America, access to western medicine is made available but generally far too costly, so reliance on imported home flora is again paramount – a part in which herbal teas play a vital role. A physician, often on site in the herbalist shop or grocer's store, will write a prescription and give it to the druggist who will weigh and place the measured herbs into a package. The patient will then take the package home and boil the herbs as prescribed in an amount of water for a specified length of time.

Of course, the drinking of herbs to the Chinese does not seem 'odd' or 'different', and their general oriental and spiritual understanding allows herbs to slip easily into the whole pattern of their lives. Knowing that the herb tea will not just correct the symptom but balance the Yin and Yang (positive and negative, male and female) within them, thus mobilising the body to heal itself, is all part of an ancient teaching. This eastern viewpoint may be a little difficult for those in the west to fully understand but explained in familiar terms this concept makes the role of the natural healer in this country much easier and the cure more successful, and more speedy.

The American influence

Most of the revival of interest in health, herbal teas and all things natural came from America and this is partly because it never really died from when the Chinese and Europeans started their transplant to the New World.

Their immediate need for self-sufficiency in all matters pushed them to sample the rich and new flora which surrounded them. Also, settlers included men and women who had been born during the reign of Elizabeth I and their knowledge of herbs with foods and beverages was keenly used. Added to all this was the vast storehouse of infinite knowledge that the American Red Indians had accumulated, whose information today still makes up three-quarters of European herbal medicine.

Thornham – my 'secret garden'

Just as coffee made a big comeback in the sixties with its swinging, stimulating effect, the seventies brought an opposite reaction with the flower people. It bred a generation of people passionate about love and peace and all things natural. The eighties is perhaps a distillation of these two decades, but the desire for self-protection in health and for natural products remains strong.

The teas developed by us at Thornham Herb Garden are now sold in shops all over Britain (and a few other countries besides), in brightly coloured packages. Their origins were humble and certainly the results were never quite imagined. Not being a businesswoman, it is astounding to me that our teas can now be bought in Australia and certainly destiny did not show her hand until the last moment.

Always wanting to grow herbs in a walled garden (a long-harboured dream from the book, *The Secret Garden*), luck, fortune and timing landed me in north Suffolk in the middle of East Anglia. Sitting in my wilderness-like walled garden gave me dreams for the future, its silence and great age inspiring ideas and answers after city life. Digging, raking, planting, propagating, clearing, cleaning and planning occupied my days, but chasing close behind me was the need to earn a living – and to earn it by making herbal teas.

Planting rows of catnip, lemon balm, borage, fennel, rosemary, and more, it soon looked like the early days of strip farming – except for the emerging knot garden in the centre. Countless experiments with tea blends were carried out, day and night, in the tiny kitchen of my home, a caravan (where I lived with my seven cats), after some months of waiting for electricity and mains water to arrive. As a student of herbal medicine, my efforts in that tiny kitchen taught me much instinctive knowledge of plants and showed me that the simplest way to understand herbs is to grow, eat and drink them. This basic approach has stayed with me and my enthusiasm for it has, and always will, remain.

Much help, love, encouragement and warmth from friends sustained my efforts (while locals looked on with suspicion at the witch in the garden!), but my biggest battle was to sell my blends of herbal teas, hand-packed in simple cellophane bags with a black and gold label. No one had ever sold blends of herbal teas before. Combinations of herbs with essential oils added (to replace those lost in drying) were not what the public were used to and, although the price was right, the public, or at least the shop-owners, were on the whole rather frosty. Single herbal teas were normally sold and drunk, so why the need for change? Selling just a few, I realised that my ideas were years too early, while some judged them to be far too late.

Just as despair set in, I gained a very special partner and friend. With new ideas and the prospect of a challenge, the garden resumed a new lease of life just in time. The old potting sheds were converted from packing rooms into a busy, bustling shop and offices, teas were sold over the counter and our battle against the prejudices of other shops had begun. 'We'll sell our own if they won't sell them for us' was the attitude. Setting up shop in the middle of a garden in the middle of a wood, miles from the nearest town, was not a recipe for success. However, patience, hard work, and extra monetary funding were slowly and gradually paying dividends. Soon, news of our blended teas reached the ears of those in London and a small step had been achieved.

The whole concept was developed by a continual education process as we talked to the public and the public, in turn, talked to us. Much of our time was originally spent just turning people away from the idea that herbs were cranky, if not dangerous, and educating them to understand that not only could they be beneficial but pleasant tasting. These were the people not *au-fait* with the wholefood, healthfood scene, but those used to shopping at local supermarkets, having normal family demands and with habits for drinking only tea and coffee – for umpteen generations. All people from all walks of life were candidates for our continual tea-tasting sessions and every comment was valued.

The living plant
The vast living storehouse of plants in the garden made it possible to experiment with fresh material, which has a very different taste to the dried plant. The hundreds of plant choices produced dozens of carefully blended mixtures, while every single taste and smell of every single plant was given time and thought. Beyond this fresh approach, herbs were imported from their country of origin in their dried state, as in the future we knew that our own small supplies would dwindle. In fact, they did so even quicker than we had anticipated, soon making our few cropping rows quite ineffective to keep up with demand, not to mention some drying problems (produced by the sheer volume harvested) with the unpredictable nature of our summers.

Buying in

Familiarity with rosemary from Spain, sage from Dalmatia, and mint from Morocco, besides many others, is very important to us. It is important also to know that as long as politics and natural disasters do not intrude, dried and tested herbs for certain blends are going to be continually forthcoming – for taste and for reasons of medicinal potency. Likewise, we always bought and still buy herbs at the time of their harvest, ensuring longevity on the shelf.

Handle with care – a balanced tea makes a balanced body, makes a balanced mind

Self-administration of herbal teas can be an unwise activity because without understanding the activity of herbs in detail imbalances can occur. For instance, certain organs can be unwittingly 'overworked', while symptoms are continually treated without the cause being understood. Information and help of this kind is, therefore, most important and, to make things easy, some standard general teas have been developed for all-purpose health and pleasure drinking. Otherwise, where there is doubt, the saying that a little of everything is always the safest answer. In other words, do not stick to one herb or even a mixture of six or more without knowing that a qualified herbalist has been involved. A very simple equation exists: a balanced tea makes a balanced body, makes a balanced mind.

Our herbal teas can be drunk either by using the tea-bags, which are so useful for taking to friends' houses, on holiday or simply for sheer convenience, or the loose blends can be made into a pot of tea in the normal manner. This is, of course, the way for most people who blend their own, but more on this subject will be covered in later chapters.

The production of the herbal teas in tea-bag form was a long-winded affair as, initially, the only machines capable of making the tea-bag necessitated chopping the herb to almost powder form in order to pack the mixture into the little sachets resulting in an insipid tasting tea. Technology has now advanced and the taste of the whole herb, and subsequent cups of tea, can be preserved.

There has been so much pleasure gained and exchanged in the whole venture of the herbal teas at Thornham, with people healing themselves and generally attaining better health, while finding undiscovered tastes – and we know this is an endless cycle. Thornham provides a unique opportunity for marrying the growing plant with market research.

Plant experimentation

My own experiences of plant experimentation began when I was studying horticulture at Wisley Gardens and the Royal Botanical Gardens at Kew, where other students and myself quite naturally and instinctively tasted all that was before us. This is something not to be recommended as, having eaten various herbs, we experienced hallucinations, sickness and many other states of altered consciousness, all of which were potentially very dangerous. Of course, we also experienced the beneficial and positive side of plants, but it was the more alarming experiences that taught me a cautious lesson and which has, ever since, given me a tremendously high regard for nature and her complex chemistries. One mishap cured me completely of any more spontaneous experimentation for good or bad results. This was when I foolishly chewed some cuckoo pint (*arum maculatum*) one day, the leaves of which contain prussic acid. My tongue started to swell up and, being on my own, I became incredibly worried, so I immediately made myself a cup of very strong black coffee (coffee beans should be part of any medicine cupboard) and waited for my alarming symptoms to subside. Luckily for me, they did.

My early days and experiments can be looked upon as a child who tests a parent's discipline, pushing at the barriers to see just how far they can be stretched. Age reduces the need and desire to keep on testing carelessly, giving way to understanding and respect. Helping people in a safe, quick way in our shop and surgery is the main way that strangers to the subject become initially involved with the drinking of herbal teas. It often starts with a question like: 'What can I take for my cold? It won't leave me'. However, hopefully this book will open up that experience to the many who live too far away to come and see us.

Our shop and surgery provide a base for those people needing more individual attention, giving personal tea recipes and healing advice. A venture that started with just a few rows of herbs and some grand ideas has led us down an interesting, rewarding and happy path, but we are always looking further ahead. We feel at Thornham, as do many other people now, that a new consciousness needs to be raised about 'enjoying' herbal brews. They should no longer remain in closet activity: cafés and restaurants should offer them and normal home consumption should be increased. Herbal teas are here to stay and as the word spreads from town to town and on through the country, there can be no looking back. . .

chapter two

A cultivating choice

Rather than indulging in a global horticultural extravaganza, I felt that the most important tisane plants to know about in depth were the ones that can be grown in the back gardens of the British Isles and allied climates. However, if you are curious, like me, about just where other plants grow and roughly what they look like, I will, in part, discuss those herbs used in the making of herbal teas which cannot be grown in this country.

Some of the back-garden herbs will receive more attention than others due to the fact that they are plants entirely safe to all persons and which, by their natural make-up, form the basis of daily herbal teas. Emphasis will be placed on our six most common culinary herbs – Mint, Fennel, Parsley, Rosemary, Sage and Thyme – as most people already have these growing in their gardens and, if this is not the case, then these would make an excellent start for would-be herb drinkers. There are thousands of interesting and useful herbs to taste and one only has to glance at Mrs M Grieves' wonderful book, *A Modern Herbal*, to realise this, but sound knowledge of just a few is really the best basis to becoming a home herbalist.

The growing of these plants, even if one is initially most disinterested in gardening, is very important. The reward factor of growing something that is not only attractive but useful has to be experienced to be understood. Very often, part of my treatment for patients involves getting their hands in some soil for the first time to grow parsley or alfalfa. This has produced many an unlikely gardener and given them an enjoyable pursuit in life.

Incidentally, although I look upon apples, carrots, celery and beetroot as invaluable herbs, these are not best made into a drink by way of an infusion and therefore a herbal tea. For their taste value and excellent medicinal merits, they are best juiced and drunk fresh.

A great many herbs we regard as indigenous or native to Britain were, in fact, introduced by the Romans, nettle for instance; while many more were brought in as seeds contained in ships' ballast, apart from the cargo of new plants and spices aboard the ships themselves. Wars, crusades and, later on, 'plant expeditions' changed the British flora rapidly, however the

Romans probably introduced more of what we look upon as our basic herbs than any other source.

For ease of cross reference to other chapters and the index, I will list the plants in alphabetical order, using firstly their common names and secondly their Latin titles. A great many people are rather put off by Latin (botanical) names but their connection with common names (vernacular) is much closer than people imagine. Latin names are very descriptive of the plant and, of course, ideal for their international use for which they were devised by Linnaeus in 1737. It is not surprising that herbs or useful medicinal plants have the greatest number of common names and that, in fact, most of the modern plants (introduced after the mid-seventeenth century) have only Latin tags as these were only of botanical interest and did not mean anything to local people for healing and feeding. Therefore, despise neither the common nor Latin name.

Agrimony   *Agrimonia eupatoria (Rosaceae)*
Habitat and appearance   Agrimony is common all over England but not so common in north Britain. It enjoys waste places, hedge banks and old common land. It is a perennial woody herb, growing 30–60cm high (unbranched), and has long, slender, bright yellow flowers (spikes), which bloom from June to September. The leaves are pinnate, numerous and with deeply cut edges, in a dark green. The plant has an aromatic scent which is also retained after drying.
Garden suitability   In the garden it enjoys reasonably drained soil of most types with a need for a little shade. It is ideal in a border with other taller herbs or as part of a wild garden. It is well worth growing, being perpetuated by root division in autumn.

Alfalfa   *Medicago sativa (Leguminosae)*
Habitat and appearance   Originally a native to the Mediterranean, it has now worldwide distribution, and grows particularly, in its wild form, in Canada. Not at all common in Britain, it prefers, and can be found on, dry, chalky and light, sandy soils. As a perennial of 30cm–1m (with a much-branched stem), with abundant moisture, it can form a dense, bushy growth. The leaves are pinnate, three on a stem and obovate-oblong in shape. The flowers are very pretty, violet-blue, in raceme clusters, blooming from late summer to mid-autumn.
Garden suitability   Ideal in the garden, particularly as its deep-reaching roots are nitrogen fixers. Its soil needs have been described but it is worth a try (with surprisingly good results) in most soils, particularly as it has a latish flowering period, while its leaves can be cut and re-cut for use throughout the season. The plant may be more familiar to those sprouting the seed in jam jars for use in salads (this seed can easily continue in the soil

for full maturity). However, whichever way this plant is grown, grown it certainly must be!

Allspice   *Pimento officinalis (Myrtaceae)*
Habitat and appearance   Also indigenous to the West Indian islands and South America. However, in this country it graces only greenhouses of botanical gardens or the very green-fingered, requiring 'stove' conditions. It is a tree that bears fruit after three to four years, which is green and turns reddish-brown on drying.
Garden suitability   For the dedicated large greenhouse owner only.

Aloe vera   *Aloe vera or aloe perryi or aloe ferox (Liliaceae)*
Habitat and appearance   A succulent, liliaceous perennial, forming clusters of stemless, fleshy, bright green leaf blades with very faint white specks, found mostly in America (California) in the wild. Some species from Africa and the Caribbean have prickly margins to the leaves and produce woody stems, bearing erect spikes of yellow, orange or red flowers all year round.

Aloe vera   *Lemon balm*

Garden suitability Aloe vera is easily grown as a house plant in sandy, stony soil with some nutritive soil added. It spreads fairly rapidly, giving off underground stems producing new young plants, which can be prised away and re-potted to produce more.

Anise *Pimpinella anisum (Umbelliferae)*

Habitat and appearance Native to Egypt, Greece and Crete, it spread to parts of Europe, including Britain, in the Middle Ages. It is a dainty plant, about 45cm high, with feathery, bright green leaflets. It has umbelliferous-looking white flowers from mid to late summer.

Garden suitability As an annual, this plant requires patience, enjoying light, dry soil in a sunny position (planted out in May). The seed will only ripen in a really hot summer, but the leaves are equally useful.

Balm, Lemon *Melissa officinalis (Labiatae)*

Habitat and appearance Previously a native to southern Europe, it is now naturalised over most of Britain, indeed I have found it growing in Wales, Yorkshire, East Anglia and all over the south of England, thus proof of an early introduction. Like all *labiatae*, it has a square stem. It is a perennial with a short root stock. Its branchy stems grow 30–60cm high and die down in the winter. Its tiny pairs of ovate leaves produce the strongest lemon smell of the plant, while its white-yellow bunches of tiny flowers bloom from June to October.

Garden suitability Balm grows incredibly easily in any soil but it particularly enjoys a moist, slightly shady situation; it sets seed quite freely, otherwise it can be root-divided in autumn (October). If you are a bee lover, this is a good choice.

Bergamot *Monarda didyma (Rustaceae)*

Habitat and appearance It is a perennial, approximately 60cm high, with protruding fragrant rootlets which die down in winter. Its square, hard stems produce its flamboyant scarlet flowers in large heads at the top, which are encircled by pale green leaflets and red-green bracts. Down the stem it has pairs of dark green leaves.

Garden suitability Bergamot really only does well and multiplies in moist, light soils, however it will grow in most soils but often becomes stunted and unhappy, especially if it receives too much sun. Its creeping roots make ideal 'Irishman's cuttings' by root division in autumn. Because it is so fragrant and ornamental, it is well worth growing.

Betony, Wood *Stachys officinalis (Labiatae)*

Habitat and appearance As its name suggests, this is a wild woodland plant, common in England though not the rest of Britain. It is perennial with a

13

thick, woody root. The stems rise from 30–60cm, but are very slim, while its leaves grow in pairs (broadish and oblong) down the stem but mostly from the base where they are more heart-shaped. It is these leaves that contain the bitter, aromatic oil in gland sacs. The top of the stem produces the rich purplish-red whorls of flowers forming the dense, dumpy spike during July and August.

Garden suitability Not very easily tamed in a garden, except in a wild situation which is shady and slightly moist. However, it is very attractive and makes excellent ground cover. Propagate by root division in autumn.

Blessed thistle *Cnicus benedictus (Compositae)*

Habitat and appearance As a native to the Mediterranean it has been introduced to many countries and grows in Britain, tolerating most soils. In the USA it has naturalised itself. It is an annual, spiky and thistle-looking (branched), growing to 70cm. Its lanceolate leaves dentated with spines on each tooth are dark green and white-veined. Partially concealed within spiny bracts, it has mid-yellow flowers, which appear from July to late September.

Garden suitability Reasonably easy to cultivate, it is not really a plant one would wish to flourish, beyond having one or two (space being plentiful), due to its spiky nature. However, it is a very attractive plant.

Borage *Borago officinalis (Boraginaceae)*

Borage

Habitat and appearance It is a hardy annual and, therefore, in slight winters a biennial. The plant grows to 45cm, and has a sturdy, hollow, round (branched) stem, while the whole plant is covered in rough white hairs. The leaves are alternate, being long and broad in shape (oval/pointed). The colour of the leaves, deep green, makes a beautiful frame for the startling bright blue, star-shaped flowers with their prominent black anthers. Autumn-sown seed flowers in May while spring-sown seed flowers in June – flowering lasts for two or three months.

Garden suitability Borage is happy in most soils and situations and, left to its own devices, it sets seed very freely. It is definitely worth garden space for its attractive, cheering nature, especially as blue flowers are relatively uncommon.

Buckwheat   *Fagopyrum esculentum (Polygonaceae)*
Habitat and appearance   Now naturalised in Britain (the Romans probably introduced it), it also grows in Asia and is cultivated worldwide. It is a herbaceous plant with a knotted stem, round and hollow, mostly green, tinged red occasionally. The lateral branches grow out of joints which appear alternatively. The stem throws off heart-shaped or arrow-shaped leaves from alternate, opposite sides. From July to September, it produces spreading panicles of numerous white flowers which are perfumed.
Garden suitability   Easily grown from seed, it produces plenty of picking foliage, enjoying almost any soil.

Burdock (Greater)   *Arctium lappa (Compositae)*
Habitat and appearance   As a biennial it reaches very handsome proportions in its second year and can sometimes become a short-lived perennial. It resembles rhubarb and has dull, pale green, dock-shaped leaves which arise on a branched system. Its flowers are tiny and tubular, red-purple in colour, forming a disc floret which gives way to its familiar roundish burs. Its root system can reach 1m or so into the ground, being a vertical tap root.
Garden suitability   If there is a space problem in the garden this is probably not a plant to be encouraged, especially as it does grow so freely in the wild. However, it is a remarkably handsome plant and looks beautiful amongst silver foliage herbs of the same proportions, such as wormwood, southernwood.

Caraway   *Carum carvi (Umbelliferae)*
Habitat and appearance   It is a typical umbelliferae-looking plant with its umbels of tiny white flowers forming a broad, flat head from June to August. Growing from 30–60cm, it has delicately cut, feathery-looking leaves, which are aromatic when crushed. The fruits – caraway seeds – appearing after flowering, are very small, shiny and slightly curved.
Garden suitability   This is a lovely garden plant, especially as it is not only excellent for herbal teas but the leaves can be used in salads and even the root eaten as a vegetable. It grows very easily and sets seed equally so, especially on falling in the autumn. It makes a pretty plant for children to grow and use.

Catmint   *Nepeta cataria (Labiatae)*
Habitat and appearance   It is a perennial with an erect branching habit, 60–90cm high. Its many small leaves are pubescent, being grey-green in colour and whitish on the under sides (they are slightly toothed). The flowers are

15

white, dotted with purple and *labiatae* in shape – they comprise whorls which form a short spike. These bloom from July to September.

Garden suitability   In the wild this plant sets seed with tremendous ease and I have found this to be the easiest way to propagate, or from a large clump by root division in autumn. Despite its natural preference for dry, light soils, it will flourish in most and makes a very pretty plant, especially amongst silver plants or other pastel-coloured flowers and blues, like hyssop and borage.

Cayenne   *Capsicum frutescens (Solanaceae)*
Habitat and appearance   It is a shrubby perennial growing from 60cm–2m, with angular branches, long obovate leaves and white flowers, eventually producing the familiar red fruits which are small and oblong.

Garden suitability   With care and attention seed can be sown and the plant grown outside in the country in a sheltered position, in a good summer, but it is generally more successful in a greenhouse. Certainly as an unusual and interesting plant to grow, it is worth an effort.

Centaury   *Erythraea centaurium (Gentianaceae)*
Habitat and appearance   It is an annual with a fibrous root, standing 8–30cm in height. Its leaves are pale green (wedge-shaped) and shiny, clustering mostly at the base of the plant like a spreading tuft. The pairs of lance-shaped leaves grow half way up the plant, giving way to its mass of star-like flowers. These are rose-red in colour, opening only in fine weather and not after midday from July onwards.

Garden suitability   It will not grow in the garden and needs to be collected wild for medicinal purposes. However, it is worth buying the herb for tea-making purposes.

Chamomile (German)   *Matricaria recutia (Compositae)*
Habitat and appearance   It is an annual, growing to 60cm, with erect stems, much branched with very feathery leaves. The flower heads are typically compositae (daisy-like), having white florets and yellow disc florets forming the centre 'button'. The whole plant is highly aromatic.

Garden suitability   A very important garden plant as it provides good ground cover and if kept cropped can provide a carpeting effect, which when walked on releases its fragrance; ideal between stonework and gravel. However, the common chamomile, *anthemis nobilis*, is best for a lawn effect. It enjoys light, sandy soils but will grow on most.

Cherry tree (Wild)   *Prunus serotina (Rosaceae)*
Habitat and appearance   The tree grows from 15–25m and is 60cm–1m in diameter, being rough and dark. Its deciduous mid-green leaves are glossy

on the upper surface; its flowers white in erect racemes, which appear in May. Its tiny, edible but bitter fruits appear from August to September.

Garden suitability   This tree is not commercially available for buying in this country. However, select seed firms can supply seed but an 18-month stratification process is necessary. Otherwise one can graft on to *prunus avium*. As this cherry is not particularly attractive to look at, I would not suggest this as a garden choice.

Chickweed   *Stellaria media (Caryophyllaceae)*

Habitat and appearance   One of the commonest weeds, it grows practically worldwide and can be found growing almost anywhere in Britain, enjoying any soil – although it flourishes in moist, rich ones. It is a weak, procumbent plant, branching and trailing across the ground. It has juicy, soft stems, which are slightly swollen at the joints. Its leaves are in pairs and very small, pale green and smooth, with a short point at the tip (oval in shape). It has small, white, star-like flowers, starting in March through to autumn. Many people find it difficult to identify this plant but its distinguishing feature is a line of hairs that runs up the stem on one side, then crosses over to the other once it reaches a pair of leaves.

Garden suitability   This plant will not wait to be considered 'suitable' – it will just simply arrive and thrive on being cut for its use in season-long salads. To obtain very succulent and fast growing specimens, I deliberately allow it to go rampant in my greenhouse. It sows seed very freely.

Cinnamon   *Cinnamomum zeylanicum (Lauraceae)*

Habitat and appearance   It is an evergreen reaching 7–10m, with a thick, pale, smooth bark and many-branched. The young shoots are greeny-orange while the leaves are petiolate and leathery when mature. The flowers are small, white and hang in panicles which then produce fruit. The whole plant smells spicy. Commercial cinnamon comes from the dried inner bark of the shoots, called 'sticks', and also from the bark, which is superior.

Garden suitability   Obviously it cannot be grown in our climate, but it can be seen in various botanical gardens: the Royal Botanical Gardens and Kew, in London, for instance.

Clover (Red)   *Trifolium pratense (Leguminosae)*

Habitat and appearance   Clover is a short duration perennial; the many stems can grow from 30–60cm, coming from a branched system. The whole plant is slightly hairy, having ovate, trifoliate leaves. The flowers are rosy-purple, occasionally white and they form dense clusters from June to October; they are slightly fragrant.

Garden suitability   This really is a wild plant or an agricultural fodder crop, however, receiving it into the garden is an easy matter, making very attractive and useful mid-height ground cover. Grow from seed in the spring like the field system.

Coltsfoot   *Tussilago farfara (Compositae)*

Habitat and appearance In February, a single (woolly but scaled) stem arises, bearing a (*compositae*) yellow flower shielded partially in reddish bracts. When these have died down, the leaves appear one or two months later on longish stems, being large, dark and furry, and almost whitish and furred on the underside, 10–18cm wide.

Garden suitability This plant, especially if given moist or even water-logged conditions, will thrive to the point of becoming a nuisance in a garden, however it does not become quite so rampant on dry soils. Root division is probably the easiest way to propagate and certainly it is a delightful plant to have, with its bright yellow flowers bringing colour in the grey days of February.

Comfrey   *Symphytum officinale (Boraginaceae)*

Comfrey

Habitat and appearance Symphytum officinale has whitish, creamy-yellow flowers which bloom from April to May right through the summer. These flowers are much larger than all the other comfrey species, as well as other white ones. The flowers form racemes in pairs (scorpoid in shape) and they are in one-sided clusters and decrease in size as they taper down the many-branched stems. The stems, 60–90cm, are angular, hollow and bristle, with hairs. The leaves, dark and green, broad/ovate and again covered in hairs, cause itching and blistering at certain times of the season when touched.

Garden suitability This plant should be encouraged in the garden if only to expand its dwindling numbers. It is extremely pretty and can be easily divided by root division in the autumn. Any soil will produce results, but if very dry then well-rotted manure will encourage its efforts. Most comfreys are good for tisane purposes, especially the ones raised by Henry Doubleday – which are high in the B_{12} vitamins: 'Bocking 14', for instance.

Coriander   *Coriandum satiuum (Umbelliferae)*

Habitat and appearance Indigenous to the Mediterranean and Caucasian areas and now native to many temperate climates. Small, glabrous, solid-stemmed, hardy annual. It has pinnate lower leaves, cleft and lobed, while the upper ones – which appear later on in the season, with the fruit – are finely dissected and quite different in appearance. Small, flat, compound umbels of white and reddish flowers appear from mid-summer to autumn, followed by brownish, roundish fruit, which ripens to become spicy and aromatic – coriander seed.

Garden suitability   Will grow easily from seed (buy a packet) in this country and will easily self-seed in following years, if not disturbed. It prefers a sheltered position, full sun and dry soil.

Dandelion   *Taraxacum officinale (Compositae)*

Habitat and appearance   It has a thick, dark brown tap root which, when cut into, has a milky-white core and outer core. Directly from the root rises a rosette shape of the toothed leaves. This arrangement and funnel shape of the centre leaves directs all available water straight to the root. From the leaves arise purplish (hollow and thin) stalks which bear single heads of flowers. Each bloom is made up of numerous strap-shaped florets, bright yellow, almost golden. These bloom from early spring till late autumn, which, incidentally, makes it an important bee plant. However, the flowers only fully open in fine weather and good sunshine. The matured flower head decays to become a plumed seed head like a gossamer ball which, when blown, disperse very readily, each seed having its own parachute.

Garden suitability   As a major medicinal plant, this plant is now gaining popularity as a vegetable or salad crop, using the roots as the former but more often the leaves as the latter. Apart from this, they really are delightful and make a very pretty decorative edge to a salad or herb garden. Dandelion thrives on nitrogen-rich soils above 200m in altitude.

Devil's Claw   *Harpagophytum procumbens (Pedaliceae)*

Habit and appearance   Grows naturally in the Kalahari Desert and Namibia. The plant has trumpet-shaped blossoms, which are red-violet in colour. It grows in red, sandy soil, sending down deep roots, but its top growth only appears in March/April if there has been enough rain, when luscious leaves are produced. These form a rosette shape around the root, giving off juicy green tendrils; when these dry up, they become extremely hard, tough and claw-like in their grip. The form is, roughly, a finger-like tendril (armed with thorns), shaping a lower rosette and bent upwards. This strange form, once dried up, grips its seeds (the size of a hand) and only pliers will release them. Tubers are arranged on the roots, being similar to a potato plant, and these store water, necessary for the plant in times of drought. The root itself is soft and yellowish-white.

Garden suitability   Definitely not.

Dill   *Anethum graveolens (Umbelliferae)*

Habitat and appearance   It is a typical umbelliferous-looking plant, reaching 1m in a season (being annual). It is somewhat similar to fennel, though simpler in arrangement, having a spindly root and only one stem, bearing a single head composed of flat umbels of numerous pale yellow flowers. The whole plant is aromatic, particularly its seeds which appear in late summer. Its leaves are feathery mid-green with linear leaflets.

Garden suitability   This makes a lovely plant, and if massed together hold each other up without any form of staking, making a lovely sight either in a wild garden or herbaceous border. Easy to grow, it does best sown by seed in spring, either directly sown or in a seed tray. After this, it self-seeds abundantly but the seed is only viable for three years.

Dock, Yellow   *Rumex crispus (Polygonaceae)*

Habitat and appearance   The root goes very deep into the ground and is thick and unforked. The stem is 30–90cm high and branched, while the leaves are dark green, curled and 15–25cm long. Like most docks and sorrels it has a flower spike made up of tiny green and reddish-pink flowers which turn a rusty yellow in autumn – hence its name.

Garden suitability   Not really something one might want to grow in the garden for its visual appearance, however, it has its own beauty and I especially like the flower spike. Once established by root division in spring or autumn it will be hard to eradicate! It is a very useful plant for medicinal purposes and invaluable in tisanes.

Echinacea   *Echinacea angustifolia (Compositae)*

Habitat and appearance   It has striking rich purple flowers, from mid-summer to early autumn, forming florets around a high cone (a typical daisy shape). These produce interesting four-sided seed in late autumn. It has tapering roots, slightly spiral in shape and fibrous at the ends and, like the rest of the plant, has an aromatic (faint), sweetish smell and taste. The entire plant grows 45cm high and is slightly furry all over, with linear, veined leaves, appearing singly and sparsely up the stem.

Garden suitability   Although originally wild, it makes a very pretty garden plant, enjoying most soils but particularly dry ones. It is easily propagated by root division in spring and autumn.

Elderflower   *Sambucus nigra (Caprifoliaceae)*

Habitat and appearance   A shrub or small tree, 10m tall. The white-cream flower heads appear mid-summer and are wide and flat, made up of numerous little flowers. They cover the bush and in autumn produce purple fruits a little like redcurrants – equally as edible. The leaves are dull green, broad and veined with a strange smell.

Garden suitability   A lovely garden plant especially as a flowering, fruiting hedge which will grow tall and thick very quickly, particularly with a little pruning. Easily propagated by suckers or cuttings, enjoying any soil but loving nitrogen-rich ones.

Eyebright   *Euphrasia rostkoviana or officinalis (Scrophulariaceae)*

Habitat and appearance   A pretty annual on branched, fairly erect stems, 10–25cm high, with dark green, slightly downy and indented leaves. The white flowers, with small purple stripes and yellow flecks, appear from mid-summer to late autumn.

Garden suitability   This cannot really be cultivated as it is semi-parasitic on certain grass species and prefers calcifugous soils. However, look out for it on poor meadow land and ancient turf.

Fennel   *Foeniculum vulgar (Umbelliferae)*

Habitat and appearance   It is a hardy biennial or, more frequently and in suitable situations, a perennial. Growing 1.5–2m high, it is an erect plant (much-branched) with hollow, greeny-blue, shiny stems. It has feathery leaves and small yellow flowers on large flat terminal umbels (very like dill), comprising 15–20 rays, appearing July to August. It produces fruit and seeds in autumn, with a distinctive aniseed taste.

Garden suitability   This beautiful plant belongs to the six culinary herbs I earlier advised that one should be familiar with. Not only very ornamental if left to grow up high, it can also be kept cut to produce a constant supply of young green leaves for cooking, garnishing and herbal teas. However, the flowers and the seeds may be used in the teas if you don't wish to crop the plant. Fennel can be, and often is, grown as an annual, being easily propagated by seed, however well-drained soil and a sunny situation will produce a happy perennial.

Ginger   *Zingiber officinale (Zingiberaceae)*

Habitat and appearance   Common throughout the Far East, it is native to southeast Asia, particularly China, and is now grown commercially in most tropical countries. The familiar ginger root is, in fact, its tuberous rhizome formed on this creeping perennial plant. It has an erect reed-like stem which appears every spring, bearing narrow lanceolate leaves that die down in the autumn. It has a flowering stalk, also rising directly from the root, from which a whitish-yellow, slightly fragrant bloom grows.

Garden suitability   Obviously not climatically suitable for our gardens.

Ginseng   *Panax pseudoginseng (Chinese) (Araliaceae)*
            Panax quinquefolium (American)

Habitat and appearance   Both ginseng are native in the wild in their own countries. Once common in China, Korea and America they are less so now, becoming rare but cultivated. Chinese ginseng is a perennial, 70–90cm tall, while the American is much smaller, 10–45cm, and has a spindly root stock which produces a single erect stem, unbranched (reddish in colour) and bearing whorls of leaves; three to five, and palmate in shape. Chinese ginseng has greenish-yellow flowers and the American one, pink. They are small, few in number, on a single terminal umbel. They flower from mid-summer to late autumn and both plants produce a bright red drupe (berry) in late autumn.

Garden suitability   This can obviously not be grown in a British garden, needing damp, cool, humus-rich woodland and the correct climate, being harvested only after nine years of growing. It cannot be grown in the same place twice.

Golden Rod   *Solidago virgaurea (Compositae)*

Habitat and appearance   Out of our 80 or so species, this is the only one native to Britain, growing wild in woodlands, clearings and grasslands. It is an erect perennial growing up to 1m high with alternative, slightly pubescent furry leaves which become smaller nearer the top of the plant. The golden flowers cluster in terminal panicles, and they appear from late summer to autumn.

Garden suitability   A very pretty plant to grow and easily propagated by root division, spring and autumn. It makes an ideal herbaceous plant as it enjoys open situations but not rich soils.

Hawthorn   *Crataegus monogyna (Rosaceae)*

Habitat and appearance   Just as Culpepper said in the seventeenth century, this plant needs little description! Native to Europe, North Africa and Asia, it is common to Britain amongst our hedges and open deciduous woods. It is a shrub or smallish tree, spreading branches with thorns. Its leaves are glabrous, broad, ovate and lobed. Its flowers are white, occasionally pink or even red, and in clusters with red anthers; they appear in May. The false fruit is scarlet and oblong, each containing one stony fruit.

Garden suitability   It grows wild happily, and enjoys being planted in almost any soil, especially as a hedge.

Hibiscus   *Hibiscus sabdariffa (Malvaceae)*

Habitat and appearance   The basis of Jamaica tea, a plant native to Asia. There are many hibiscus, but this is the most popular for tisane purposes. It is an annual, reaching 2m, forming a branching, broad, bushy growth. Its stems are slightly shiny and reddish, while the leaves are ovate and undivided with small three-lobed stem leaves. The flowers are beautiful and solitary, consisting of red calyx and yellow corolla, each on a leaf axil.

Garden suitability This can be grown from seed, but it must have a tropical environment to survive.

Hops *Humulus lupulus (Cannabaceae)*

Habitat and appearance This is a British native plant and common throughout Europe. From a stout perennial root arises a thick, tough, twining stem each year, bearing heart-shaped and lobed leaves, which are dark green with finely-toothed edges. It has tiny flowers – greenish-yellow catkins arising from the axils of the leaves, which are the female flowers; while the male flowers appear on separate plants, forming loose bunches. They appear from late summer to early autumn.

Garden suitability Easily grown either by early summer cuttings or root division in spring. They make attractive heighteners if twined around wig-wam hazel poles – an idea much used in the eighteenth century. Interesting, variegated, ornamental varieties also exist.

Horehound (White) *Marrubium vulgare (Labiatae)*

Habitat and appearance Found all over Europe and indigenous to Britain, it is a perennial herbaceous plant. It is particularly common to East Anglia, where cottage escapes for herb tea drinking have flourished. It is a bushy plant with quadrangular (like all *labiatae*) and branching stems. Reaching 30–45cm, it bears whitish flowers at the top of the stems; these are borne in crowded, axillary, woolly whorls, from June to September. The leaves are whitish-green with felted hairs; they are rather wrinkled and appear in opposites up the stem.

Garden suitability This is a pleasant plant, only flowering after two years, however; it is hardy and easily grown. It will flourish on most soils but enjoys dry, poor soil the most. It is best propagated by root division in spring or autumn, although it can be grown from seed or cuttings.

Horsetail *Equisetum arvense (Eguisetaceae)*

Habitat and appearance A prehistoric plant, this is a British native, but its other species cover temperate northern regions. This perennial has a long creeping root system from which arise simple shoots in the spring – these are erect, jointed and brittle; the plant has no leaves. These first shoots are fertile and die just after it has shed spores later in the spring, then sterile shoots appear, bearing fronds which, in summer, produce numerous slender, jointed branches in whorls of ten or more. This class of plants is very close to ferns in make-up and propagation.

Garden suitability This plant will only thrive in wet, boggy situations if one is lucky to cultivate it. However, once it is established in an area, it is very difficult to eradicate because of its rampant underground root system.

Kava-Kava   *Piper methysticum (Piperaceae)*
Habitat and appearance   Coming from the same family as black pepper (*piper nigram*) and cubeb (*piper cubeba*), it looks similar. It is a perennial climbing shrub from Polynesia.
Garden suitability   Cannot be grown in this country.
***Note:* Kava-Kava should not be taken long term.**

Kelp (or Bladderwrack)   *Fucus vesiculosus (Fucaceae)*
Habitat and appearance Common on north west Atlantic coastlines, especially Scotland, Norway and North America. It is a perennial seaweed, consisting of a leathery, thin, branching, brownish-green thallus (finger-like projections). It attaches itself to rocks by means of a woody 'stripe' and discoid holdfast. Running the length of the plant, air vesicles are borne in pairs. It terminates in strong, globose fructifications with air in them.
Garden suitability   Definitely not!

Lavender (English)   *Lavendula vera or angustifolia (Labiatae)*
Habitat and appearance   There are many lavender species of which the English is but one; this one, like most, being native to southern Europe and the Mediterranean. It is a perennial sub-shrub reaching 30–90cm. It has a much-branched, irregular stem, short, thick and wooded at the base. Leaves are narrow, lanceolate, greeny-grey and slightly tomentose (furry). It's a generally aromatic plant, particularly the flowers, which appear from mid-summer to early autumn. They show spikes some 10mm long and are grey-blue in colour.
Garden suitability   Enjoying well-drained, slightly sandy conditions (but also poor soil), it needs sunshine – at least four hours per day. It is one of the hardier species and ideal for the garden, flourishing to greater heights under cultivation.

Lemon tree   *Citrus limonum (Rutaceae)*
Habitat and appearance   Native to northern India, it is widely cultivated in Mediterranean countries. It is a small, straggling tree, 3–4m high, with an irregular branching system and slightly shiny ovate-oval leaves. It has solitary five-petalled flowers, highly fragrant and slightly waxy to look at, white and tinged pink outside. Its famous fruit is a frequent addition to herb teas.
Garden suitability   It cannot be grown as a garden plant.

Lime (Linden tree)   *Tilia cordata (Tiliaceae)*
Habitat and appearance   As a European native it is very ancient as a 'tea-making' tree, using its blossom. It is a deciduous tree, occasionally a shrub, reaching 20–40m high, and its trunk is straight and powerful. The leaves are

orbicular and serrate while the tea blossom is yellowish-white in mostly pendulous cymes of five to ten flowers, which appear from mid to late summer. In the autumn, globose fruits are produced, each having two helicopter-wing-like leaflets to help flight for propagation purposes.

Garden suitability This makes a lovely garden tree but it does need quite a lot of space and its height would shade a small garden. It enjoys sandy or stony soils; interestingly it is often used as a street tree, even with its offensive, dripping, sticky secretions in spring, caused by a burrowing bug. For this reason also it is best planted well away from the house, patio or car!

Liquorice *Glycyrrhiza glabra (Leguminosae)*

Habitat and appearance Native to southern Europe and southern Asia, it was introduced to central and western Europe (Britain included, especially Pontefract in Yorkshire) some 400 years ago. It is an herbaceous perennial with a vertical tap root and a penetrating branching system. It has horizontal rhizomes just below the soil surface which spread very quickly, providing self-propagation from the leaf buds and second-year shoots which freely appear. It is this entire underground system which provides liquorice. Above soil, it has graceful, delicate foliage, pinnate in arrangement, having leaflets on a mid-rib. From the leaf axils appear small, pale blue, purple-blue and sometimes yellowy-white flowers. Typical pea-family-shaped flowers appear, which in the autumn produce tiny, brownish pea-pods.

Garden suitability An ideal garden plant, especially as it is beneficial for soil quality and structure due to its penetrative root system, but it does enjoy rich, manured soils. Early autumn or spring is the time to plant pieces of its runners or side roots (with eye buds intact); plant just beneath soil surface.

Marigold *Calendula officinalis (Compositae)*

Habitat and appearance A native to south Europe, it grows very occasionally wild in this country, but more normally in gardens for its pretty flower, thriving in most soils. Only the common deep orange variety is medicinal. It has pale green leaves and golden-orange flowers, which appear from late spring well into late autumn, being killed by the first frosts. Such a familiar flower to everyone hardly needs a better description.

Garden suitability Old herbalists of the sixteenth century grew this flower for its use in cookery, medicine and for its beauty; we should do the same. Producing copious seed, it sows itself, increasing from year to year if left undisturbed, though, in fact, it is an annual.

Marjoram (Wild) *Origanum vulgare (Labiatae)*

Habitat and appearance There are quite a few species of marjoram and all are medicinally beneficial. Common throughout Europe, this one used to flourish wild in this country but is now cultivated and rarely seen in the wild. It is a bushy, aromatic, slightly hairy perennial, born on a horizontal root stock. It has small, petiolate, pointed, broadly ovate leaves, occasionally toothed, appearing opposite and decussate up the stem. The flowers are rose-purple, sometimes pinky-white, born on bracteoles (purplish), ending in short spikes or clusters (*corymbose*) in late summer.

Garden suitability   It makes a lovely garden plant and is easily propagated by cuttings or by root division of a clump during spring or autumn.

Marshmallow   *Althaea officinalis (Malvaceae)*

Habitat and appearance   Native to most countries in Europe, Asia, Australia and North America; also parts of England. It is an erect hardy perennial, 1–2m high, with a few branching stems which die down in the autumn. The leaves are roundish and ovate with a toothed margin; both stem and leaves are slightly hairy. It produces five-petalled white-pink flowers from late summer to early autumn. This is followed by a flat round ('cheeses'), late-autumn fruit. It has a very tough, penetrating root system.

Garden suitability   This makes a lovely garden addition, being a delicate, attractive plant. Propagation is by seed sowing, spring or summer, or rootstock division, spring or autumn. It enjoys a light soil, yet cool roots, so the addition of compost with planting is advisable.

Meadowsweet   *Filipendula ulmaria (Rosaceae)*

Habitat and appearance   As a native to Asia and Europe it will be a familiar sight to country dwellers in Britain, lining river and stream banks. It is an attractive perennial herb, 70–125cm, with a strong, aromatic root stock and erect, reddish stems. It has alternate, acute, ovate leaves which are irregularly pinnate with two to five pairs of leaflets. These are tomentose (furred) on the underside and whitish-green on top. From the main stem arises glabrous stems, producing irregular paniculate cymes which bear sweet-smelling flowers. These are small and very dainty, being creamy-white and five-petalled with numerous long stamens. It has two flowering sessions, mid-summer and autumn, the two often running into each other.

Garden suitability   It must have wet and moist conditions. It does very well on loamy, clayish soils in shade but will tolerate most nutrient-rich soils with moisture and a little shade. This plant is really worth growing for its very pretty flowers and long season. Easily propagated by root division, spring or autumn, but tough to dig up!

Mints   Spearmint *(Mentha viridis) (Labiatae)*
Peppermint *(Mentha piperita)*
Pennyroyal *(Mentha polegium)*

This is a large family and the three major ones are mentioned above.

Spearmint *(Mentha viridis)*
This is often called garden mint and, although a common garden plant, it is not native to Britain but to the Mediterranean region. It has creeping stock roots and erect, square stems (reaching approximately 60cm high), bearing pointed, lance-shaped, slightly wrinkled, mid-green leaves. It has tiny flowers forming dense clusters, being pinky-purple and appearing mid-summer.

Peppermint *(Mentha piperita)*
A native throughout Europe, and in Britain very common in damp, wet areas in England. The stems, 50cm–1m high, are quadrangular and bear broad, smooth and finely-toothed leaves. The whorled clusters of reddish-violet flowers are born on small spikes, appearing in mid-summer.

Pennyroyal *(Mentha polegium)*
Native to Europe and Asia, and common in Britain. This is the smallest of these three mints and very different in form. It has weak prostrate stems (quadrangular in shape) extending from 5–30cm, which stem down rootlets along its length. The leaves are oval (roundish), grey-green and small. The flowers are in whorled clusters, rising in tiers like a wedding cake at each node (from which spring leaf pairs), from mid-stem to top. They flower in mid-summer, July to August, and are reddish-purple to lilac in colour.

Garden suitability   All mints in the garden are there at the owner's risk. All spread rapidly, especially if given a slightly moist or even damp-wet situation, although pennyroyal is a little less rampant. To keep the plant in check, plant either in a sunken bucket or behind a small retaining brick wall – well away from other plants, which it will swallow up.

Motherwort   *Leonurus cardiaca (Labiatae)*
Habitat and appearance   This is a European native but the only British native of the entire genus; once wild, it is now rare. A tall, slim, erect perennial, 1m tall, on a strong square stem which is branched near the base to mid-stem. The whole plant has closely set leaves, the lower ones being deeply palmate lobed and the upper ones small (three lobed). The flowers (mid-stem to tip), arranged in whorls (of 10 or so), hug the stem, forming a rocket shape. They are pale pinky-purple and very small, appearing from summer to mid-autumn, but mainly in August.
Garden suitability   Highly suitable for the garden and most attractive and unusual; really ideal in the herbaceous border as a group. Easily propagated by root division during spring and autumn; otherwise, it does self-seed and plantlets can be collected in late spring before hoeing.

Mullein, Great   *Verbasium thapsus (Scrophulariaceae)*
Habitat and appearance   Native to Europe and Asia; now naturalised in North America and Britain. Mullein has an erect, spire-shaped stem, the

27

whole plant being covered in a soft, woolly down. It is a biennial, some 2m tall, and its leaves are grey-green, which form a rosette shape in spring, being broad and ovate in form themselves. As the leaves extend up the plant to the singular spike or sometimes three or four branched ones, they become smaller. Each dense spike is made up of yellow, sessile flowers in clusters, which appear from mid-summer to late autumn.

Garden suitability   A really important garden addition, so attractive and ideal for providing height and colour. It sets seed reasonably freely, so digging up the small rosettes in spring and placing them where desired is an easy answer to propagation. Otherwise, seed should be autumn sown. Enjoys well-drained, stony, shallow soils – and warmth.

Nettles (Greater or common)   *Uritica dioica (Urticaceae)*

Habitat and appearance Native to Europe and Asia, and common throughout Britain since Roman days. A perennial, 90cm-2m tall, it has a creeping and fast-multiplying root system. Its leaves are heart-shaped, finely-toothed, on sparsely branched, bristly stems. It has green flowers, forming clusters in long, drooping racemes. Male and female flowers appear on different plants relying on wind fertilisation; they appear between June and September. The whole plant is covered with the familiar stinging hairs.

Garden suitability   This is probably a plant which does not need to be encouraged, however it is always wise to allow a patch of nettles somewhere, for spring cutting and for the general ecosystem balance in the garden.

Parsley   *Petroselinum crispum (Umbelliferae)*

Habitat and appearance   Native to the eastern Mediterranean and possibly introduced to Britain from Sardinia in 1548. The whole plant grows some 75cm high, having close, deep-curled leaves on a dark green, slim stem, which produces many single branches. There are many, many varieties, some growing very tall, some extremely short, some having deeply-frilled leaves, so large they hide a short stem, while others have very plain leaves on long stems. All have smallish, greenish-yellow flowers in wide, flat-topped umbels from mid-summer to early autumn.

Garden suitability   An eminently worthy garden plant and the third in alphabetical order of my six important culinary/medicinal herbs. Grown from seed, it enjoys partially shaded, moist, well-worked soil, and can easily be overwintered under a portable cloche. It is best re-sown each early spring, though it is a biennial or short-lived perennial.

Plantain (Common)   *Plantago major (Plantaginaceae)*

Habitat and appearance   This very British weed is native to the whole of

Two plantains

Europe, including other temperate zones, like its close relative, the species *plantago lanceolata* – ribwort. It is a perennial which grows on a short rhizome with many long, thin roots. Above the soil is a radial rosette of leaves which are obovate and slightly toothed, having a channelled footstalk; the whole leaf being deeply ribbed and veined. The flowers are inconspicuous, though numerous, they are yellow to purplish-green in colour, in dense spikes borne on long stalks rising above the leaf structure. They flower from early summer to mid-autumn.

Garden suitability   Plantain enjoys moist, loamy, nutrient-rich soils or even sandy, moist ones, but will grow in almost all soil conditions. I find it an extremely attractive plant and in a garden it reaches greater proportions, making ideal ground cover, grown alongside its ornamental cousin, *plantago major purpurea* (purple leaved and even longer).

Poke Root   *Phytolacca decandra (Phytolaccaceae)*
Habitat and appearance Indigenous to North America and most Mediterranean countries. This plant is perennial, having a large, fleshy root

29

and hollow stem. Its leaves are ovate-lanceolate and appear alternate up the stem. It is a striking plant, even though its flower has no corolla but a white calyx. However, the fruit is remarkable, covering the stem in clusters, looking like blackberries, being deep purple in colour.
Garden suitability   Cannot, sadly, be grown in this country.

Raspberry (Red)   *Rubus idaeus (Rosaceae)*
Habitat and appearance   Growing wild in large areas in Britain, it is native to parts of Europe and Asia. This shrubby plant has stems which are erect, drooping down at the top, 90cm-1.5m tall. Most of the plant is covered in prickles, though some have none at all. The leaves are obovate, slightly toothed, grey-white and tomentose underneath and deep green on top. They form three or five leaflets to a stalk, like most of the rose family. It has small, droopy panicles of flowers from early to mid-summer, then the familiar cone-shaped red fruits.
Garden suitability   Having pernicious, creeping, perennial roots, this plant should not be left unattended! However, grown for its fruit-bearing qualities it is an essential, given the room. It naturally enjoys moist, light soil, bulging with nutrients, but it will thrive in most conditions.

Rosehip (Dog Rose)   *Rosa-canina (Rosaceae)*
Habitat and appearance   Native to Europe, North Africa and Asia, it is a very common sight in British hedgerows. It is a climbing, trailing perennial shrub, gaining heights of 1–3m. The whole plant is covered in prickles, but in mid to late summer it is also covered in large white or pale pink, sweet-smelling flowers. These are then followed by 15mm-long fleshy, scarlet fruits (hips) in autumn. Its leaves are alternate, ovate and serrate and slightly acute, and look like all others of the rose family.
Garden suitability   Easily grown from seed, this is a rampant plant, especially if given rich, loamy soil. It makes a wonderfully thick hedge, though prickly! It is frequently cultivated for its use as a root stock for grafting other rose varieties.

Rosemary   *Rosmarinus officinalis (Labiatae)*
Habitat and appearance   Native to the Mediterranean coast. This shrubby, aromatic and evergreen perennial reaches 1–2m, more or less depending on the species. With age, the plant becomes more woody. Its leaves are linear, dark green above and pale beneath, while the flowers are pale blue and small, appearing from late spring to early summer.
Garden suitability   Rosemary is the fourth of the six important culinary herbs in this chapter and is an old favourite throughout history. It succeeds best in light, slightly dryish soils which should be sheltered and facing

south if possible; ideal at the base of a wall. Rosemary can be propagated by seeds, cuttings and layerings, but the two latter are perhaps the easiest way to produce plants. This is a plant never to be without, even if it means growing it in a pot and bringing it in over winter in colder regions.

Sage (Common) *Salvia officinalis (Labiatae)*

Habitat and appearance Native to southern Europe, especially the Mediterranean, though cultivated for many centuries in Britain, France and Germany. Sage grows 40–80cm high and has a shrubby appearance, having a woody base stem which branches out into more wiry stems (woody when young). The leaves are set in pairs on the stem and are grey-green in colour, again soft and downy. The flowers blossom in August and are violet-blue in colour, arranged in whorls on terminal spikes.

Garden suitability   No more suitable a garden plant and, of course, ranking one of the 'culinary six'. It enjoys a warm and rather dry border, doing best in a partially shaded situation but will, however, flourish almost anywhere (not under trees). Although a perennial, it does degenerate in three or four years, so cuttings should be taken at these times to ensure continual stocks. This highly aromatic plant is just one of many species and cultivars, some with red leaves, some golden, some variegated, and many more.

St John's wort *Hypericum perforatum (Hypericaceae)*

Habitat and appearance   Native to temperate regions of Europe and western Asia, being fairly common throughout Britain; now naturalised in America and Australia. *Hypericum* spreads rapidly by its long runners from which arise erect stems, producing small branches at the top. This perennial grows from anything between 20–65cm tall, depending on the soil. It has oblong or linear leaves, in opposites; if held up to the light, tiny translucent oil spots can be seen, alluding to its name *perforatum* – perforated. Its flowers are deep yellow, star-shaped and five-petalled, borne on many flowered terminal cymes. They appear from late summer to autumn.

Garden suitability   This wild plant will very often sow itself in the garden but, if not, it is very worthy of inclusion for its gay yellow flowers. It is easily propagated by root division with its many runners, during autumn.

Sarsaparilla (Jamaican) *Smilax ornata (Liliaceae)*

Habitat and appearance   Native to central America, particularly Costa Rica. It has a twining, woody stem which is prickly, and paired tendrils which help it to cling. Leaves are obovate, oblong and pointed (30cm long) with accentuated veins; they are alternate up the stem. It has beautiful greenish-white flowers which are small and star-shaped, hanging in clusters.

Garden suitability   This is certainly not a garden plant for these Isles.

Sassafras   *Sassafras albidum (Lauraceae)*
Habitat and appearance   North American native. An aromatic, deciduous tree, reaching 30m. Leaves are lobed or entire. Clustered greenish-yellow flowers on racemes. Has dark blue fruit.
Garden suitability   Growing wild in America, it can be grown in this country and has been in the past, though it is not common. It has very attractive autumn colours.

Scullcap (Virginian)   *Scutellaria laterifolia (Labiatae)*
Habitat and appearance   There are several scullcaps, this being the best one and ably grown in Britain, while other species are actually native. It is native to America. It is a perennial plant, growing 60–90cm high, its foliage dying down in the autumn. It has distinctive square stems which are branched, having opposite, downy leaves which are oblong and tapering, heart-shaped at the base. The flowers appear in July and are on one-sided terminal racemes, being a delicate shade of blue. The plant produces seed in autumn.
Garden suitability   Loving any garden soil (not too rich), *scutellaria* species do best in sunny, open situations. Grown from seed they can be planted out in spring, otherwise root division can be used from older plants (they generally don't last much longer than three years), again in spring. A very attractive and unusual plant.

Thyme (Garden)   *Thymus vulgaris (Labiatae)*
Habitat and appearance   As an 'improved' or cultivated form of the wild thyme from Europe and a near relative to our British wild thyme (*thymus serpyllum*), it is not native to anywhere. It is an aromatic sub-shrub which has woody stems and, although a perennial, can dwindle in vitality after three to five years of growth. It reaches 10–30cm, and has numerous, round, hard stems, which branch out. The leaves are tiny and linear-elliptic, grey-green in colour, and set in pairs. The flowers terminate the branches in whorls of dense or sparse inflorescences, and are lilac to white, flowering from May to August.
Garden suitability   The sixth of the culinary herbs, it is probably the most widely known, alongside its very many other species and hybrids. Propagation can be achieved by cuttings, root division or seed, but the easiest method is to prise away a piece of the plant which is attached to some root (peaty soil makes this easier), i.e. an 'Irishman's cutting'. Easy to propagate, it can be grown almost anywhere (even in very cold climates as an annual) and should definitely adorn your own garden, especially as it is one of the first herbs to flower in the season, attracting bees and butterflies. It enjoys almost uncultivated ground and grows on or near dry walls or stony land, becoming very hardy. Lighten heavy soil with grit.

Sassafras

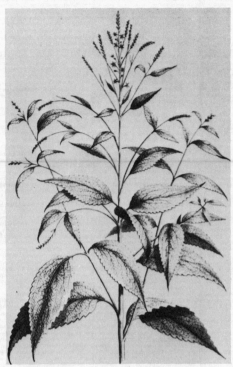

Vervain

Verbena, Lemon   *Lippia citriodora (Verbenaceae)*
Habitat and appearance   Native to Chile and Peru, it is now widely cultivated in Europe. This is a deciduous perennial shrub and the whole plant abounds with fragrant, volatile oil. The leaves are particularly fragrant, pale green, of medium length and lanceolate with parallel veins. They are arranged in threes along the stems, which form a sparse branched system. Its height varies from 30cm–3.5m, depending on the age of the specimen. It flowers in August, producing terminal panicles made up of many small flowers, which are pale purple.
Garden suitability   If a sheltered, dry, southerly aspect exists, especially against a wall, this plant can survive a British winter in the middle to southern counties. Otherwise, it is best grown in a large clay pot and brought in in winter. It particularly enjoys light, gritty soil and rewards a correct environment with a heavenly scent.

Vervain   *Verbena officinalis (Verbenaceae)*
Habitat and appearance   Native to the Mediterranean but well-established elsewhere and reasonably common as a roadside herb in Britain. This is a

33

perennial on angular, ribbed, erect stems, all to a height of 40–80cm. It is a loosely-branched, sparsely-leafed plant, the leaves being opposite and cut into toothed lobes. It has small, pale lilac flowers at the tips of long stalks which appear from summer to late autumn.

Garden suitability   An interesting plant, it is very easy to grow and best propagated by seed. It enjoys most soils but does like full sun.

Violet   *Viola odorata (Violaceae)*

Habitat and appearance   Common throughout Britain, wild and cultivated. The plant has heart-shaped leaves, arising from creeping rhizomes. The flowers appear from February to April (although mine seem to flower from autumn, all winter, through to spring) and they are generally deep purple, having five sepals and five petals. The whole plant has an unmistakably beautiful perfume. It reaches just a few centimetres in height, and thrives in most soils.

Garden suitability   For the fact that this plant starts to flower during the bleak periods of the year and for its beautiful scent and good looks, it must be grown by all, especially as it takes up so little space. It enjoys most garden soils from slightly chalky, to sandy, to loamy. Although it is suggested that its own overcrowding weakens its flowering capabilities, I have never found this to be so. Propagation is easiest by root division in spring or autumn.

Note: I have not included this in the table of dried specimens as the leaves of violets should and must be used fresh for tea-drinking (medicinal) purposes, while the violets do not retain their exquisite scent on drying.

Yarrow   *Achillea millefolium (Compositae)*

Habitat and appearance   Native to Europe and some temperate regions. It is a perennial with a stoloniferous 'matting' root system which is far-creeping. The stems are angular and rough to the feel, slightly furrowed. The leaves are alternate, bipinnate and linear, being finely cut giving a feathery appearance, hence its name *millefolium*. It flowers from June to September, having flattened terminal loose heads made up of many small daisy-like flowers, pale lilac-rose or white in colour.

Garden suitability   This plant quickly colonises, due to its spreading root system and can even be mown into a lawn! Propagation is naturally by root division, while it enjoys most soils. It is a pretty plant and, alongside its other species, makes an attractive herbaceous addition.

chapter three

Your garden of miracles
Town and country planting

Planning a garden of miracles might conjure up Chinese and Japanese gardens with all their elegance, peace and age-old beauty, or perhaps your image is of sultry Victorian summer days with tea on the lawn. However, the idea can not only advance into modern times but bring with it a new outlook, that is, of having the tea plants growing around you, in an intimate corner, combining their growing with their drinking. Room permitting, one can landscape on the grand scale using all the herbs mentioned in Chapter two suitable for the garden or, more likely, just pick a small selection, particularly those that will not invade or advance too rapidly. For those with very little space or no garden at all, perhaps living in towns and cities, then pots, tubs and hanging baskets are an exciting answer.

Japanese gardens

An attempt at building a Japanese garden is an adventurous one, however the connection between the drinking of tea and of gardens is stronger in no other culture or country. In the fifteenth century, the rite of tea drinking became highly ceremonial, and the one or two garden rooms dedicated to this purpose and the garden surrounding them were given more and more attention until they became the most beautiful parts of the grounds. Attention should be paid to the fact that whatever the existing terrain, water should flow from east to west. Stones may need to be brought in, often being very heavy. Years of careful tending and training, with attention to minute detail, are the key to the beauty of a Japanese garden – but if you feel this is too ambitious, let me bring you closer to home.

Knot gardens

Knot gardens were one of the earliest forms of deliberate garden planning in Britain, becoming fashionable in the late fifteenth and sixteenth centuries. Their hallmark is the knotting and interflowing effect of the shapes, with herbs spilling from the constraints of clipped hedges and

35

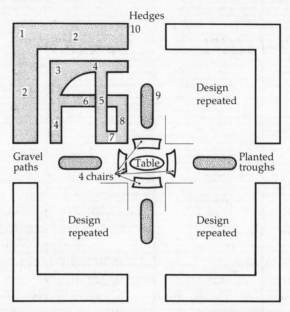

Hedges

Design repeated

Gravel paths

Table

4 chairs

Planted troughs

Design repeated

Design repeated

1. Bronze fennel *(foeniculm vulgare purpureum)*
   Perennial, height 60–90 cm.
   Rich soil, warm. Flowers July to Sept.

2. Golden lemon balm *(melissa officinalis variegatum)*
   Perennial, height 60–70 cm.
   Rich soil, shelter, sun or shade.
   Flowers July to Sept.

3. Hyssop *(hyssopus officinalis)*
   Perennial, height 50–60 cm.
   Sunny situation. Flowers June to Sept.

4. Sage, common *(salvia officinalis)*
   Perennial, height 45–50 cm.
   Sunny situation. Flowers July to Sept.

5. Marigold *(calendula officinalis)*
   Annual, height 30–40 cm.
   Full sun. Flowers June to Nov.

6. Pineapple mint *(mentha suaveolens variegata)*
   Perennial, height 30–45 cm.
   Sun or shade. Flowers August to Sept.

7. Parsley, curly *(petroselinum crispum)*
   Biennial, height 15–20 cm.
   Sun or partial shade. Flowers June to August

8. Chamomile *(anthemis nobilis)*
   Perennial, height 15–20 cm.
   Sunny situation. Flowers July to August

9. Trough plant:-
   Lemon verbena *(aloysia triphylla)*
   Half hardy perennial; height 60 cm. plus;
   (brings pots in over winter)
   Sun and shelter. Flowers July

10. Box *(busus sempervirens)*
    Perennial, height – keep low clipped

The knot – a formal tea garden

bordered paths. Intimacy and intrigue are the feelings aroused from strolling visitors, and colour and scent play an important role.

It is at the very centre of this geometric pattern that I have placed a sheltered, enclosed tea area with a table and four seats. The siting for this usurps the traditional centre-piece of a box tree or sun-dial, with a change also in the size of the knot garden from the grand proportions of the fifteenth and sixteenth centuries. The design, which includes room for a small, round table and four garden chairs, can be created comfortably in a space 4.5 × 4.5m.

Some geometric designs for knot gardens

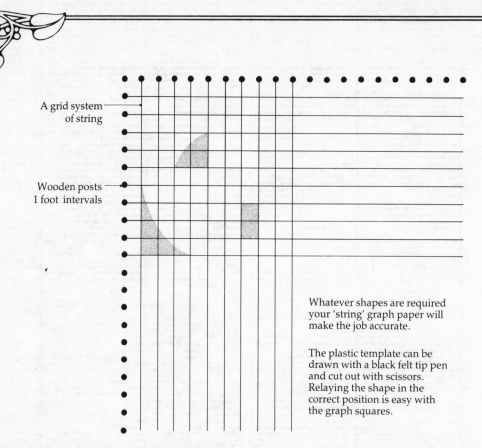

A grid system of string

Wooden posts 1 foot intervals

Whatever shapes are required your 'string' graph paper will make the job accurate.

The plastic template can be drawn with a black felt tip pen and cut out with scissors. Relaying the shape in the correct position is easy with the graph squares.

How to draw shapes on to the soil

Translating this shape from paper to soil can be an easy task if certain rules are followed. First of all, site it in a well-considered spot – sunny, near the house, in a quiet corner – and the ground must be level, dug, raked and allowed to settle. Then a string grid should be laid down so that the repeated pattern remains exact. To make things simple, a plastic template, cut from polythene sheets, produces a quick and efficient way to duplicate the major shapes.

Laying paths and making edges or hedges is the next task; gravel is the cheapest answer to a path or, if money permits, beautiful stone or brickwork. Again, bricks can create the low edges you need, laid at 45 degree angles.

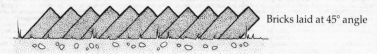

Bricks laid at 45° angle

Brick edging

Otherwise, a low herb hedge of lavender, rosemary, or sage can be used and, while needing the attention of the shears three or more times a year in order to keep a trim shape, the clippings can be dried for winter teas.

An informal tea garden

As a complete contrast to the symmetry of the knot tea garden, we now look at a more pliable, relaxed environment which can be handled in many ways. Again the site must be carefully chosen, but a level one is not a necessity, in fact a hollow or incline would add more character. There should be at least four hours of sunshine a day and preferably in the afternoon for the 'tea ritual'. A section of the tea garden might easily be slightly damp or even have a stream nearby where scarlet-headed flowers of the bergamot plant could flourish with spearmint and peppermint. Otherwise, an array of herbs could jostle high and low, forming a curved, intimate space.

1. Witchhazel *(hamaemelis virginiana)*
   Perennial up to 360 cm. high.
   Rich loam, sheltered, sun. Flowers autumn.

2. Elder *(sambucus nigra)*
   Perennial 180−450 cm. high.
   Fertile dampish soil, sun. Flowers June, July.

3. Mullein, Great *(verbascum thapsus)*
   Perennial 150−250 cm. high.
   Well drained stony soil, sun.
   Flowers mid-summer to October.

4. Yarrow *(achillea millefolium)*
   Perennial 30−40 cm. high.
   Well drained soil, sun. Flowers June to August.

5. Catmint *(nepeta cataria)*
   Perennial 100−200 cm. high.
   Most soils, likes sun.
   Flowers July to Sept.

6. Marshmallow *(althaea officinalis)*
   Perennial 100−200 cm. high.
   Light soil, cool roots.
   Flowers mid-summer.

7. Rosemary *(rosmarinus officinalis)*
   Perennial 90−150 cm. high.
   Light sandy soil, sun, shelter.
   Flowers April, May, June.

8. Clover' and red *(trifolium pratense)*
   Perennial, height 70–100 cm. approx.
   Most soils, sun. Flowers June to October.

9. Peppermint *(metha piperata)*
   Perennial 200 cm. – 400 cm. high.
   Light soil, moisture. Flowers mid-summer.

10. Spearmint *(mentha viridis)*
    Perennial 200 cm. high.
    Light soil, moisture. Flowers mid-summer.

11. Bergamot *(monarda didyma)*
    Perennial, height 2' approx.
    Moist light soils, ideal by stream.
    Flowers July–Sept.

Informal herb tea garden

Here is an idea involving a wooden platform which, on a hot, dry day, could be used as a vast table with scatter cushions for comfort; the surrounding log-rounds and gravel complement the wood and make weeding easy. However, the wooden platform could just as easily be grass, perhaps on a slightly raised site. Whatever mediums are used and whether you sit on a rug or upright chairs, the feel should be busy and friendly.

The no-space tea garden

This is a popular option, even with people who have good-sized gardens, as everybody enjoys a patio or area by the house, which is dry, attractive and easily maintained.

Even if one has a width of no more than 1–1.5m this can accommodate chairs and a table and masses of pots. Most likely there will be a wall on one side from which to hang baskets or wall pots but, if not, then trellis-work and posts can provide shelter and privacy.

Pots, tubs and hanging baskets

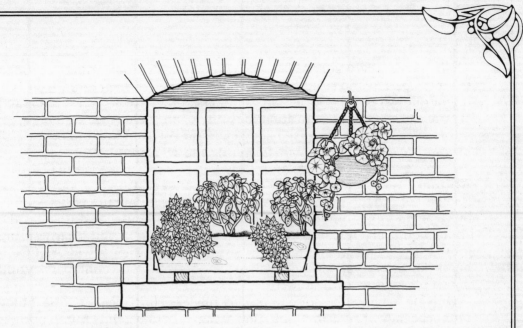

Window-box herb garden

The window-box

Of course, if one has a second-storey flat, then a window-box is the single answer and here rosemary can stretch, thyme can tumble, alfalfa can be grown as a short-lived annual and parsley can flourish amongst them all.

The correct soil for each herb was discussed in Chapter two and, where possible, when putting the chosen herbs into pots, wooden tubs or hanging baskets, those same soils should apply. However, there are obvious difficulties, that is, that often several plants are chosen, all needing varying soils and differing degrees of moisture. So always combine herbs which enjoy light soils, good drainage and lots of sunshine – for example, in a tub of rosemary, thyme, lavender and sage, don't plant borage which would struggle, be stunted and eventually die through lack of water. Moisture-loving herbs, often equated with generous root systems, such as borage, comfrey, bergamot and mint, must be planted in a container that is at least an old horse trough and well within reach of a tap. For both dry and moisture-loving plants, any container should have good drainage (water-logging kills as swiftly as lack of water) and this means filling with pebbles, stones and gravel, to a depth of one-tenth of the container.

Food for life
For the plants to grow successfully and produce the beautiful fragrances and flavours that have stirred us to grow them in the first place, they must receive the same nutritional conditions as their garden soil counterparts.

Again, for dry, light-soiled plants this is really not a problem and very often the more barren and scant the conditions, the better the fragrance of, say, thyme. However, hyssop, lemon balm, pineapple sage, lemon verbena and comfrey all appreciate extra attention and, for an overall care system to suit most tastes, I would suggest a liberal addition of leaf mould to provide all necessary elements for growth, flowering and seed production.

Autumn, winter and spring; care and conservation

Pot, basket and tub-grown herbs can be easily protected from frost, simply by removing them into a shed, hallway or greenhouse, and this has the added bonus of stretching the season of the herbs, providing early spring growth and a late autumn growth. If care is taken, then a winter of fresh herbs is possible with a warm kitchen window-sill where mint, parsley and pineapple sage never die down.

Outside, all must be done to protect the less hardy against frost if they cannot be moved, and anything from sacking, bound gently round upright herbs, to mini-cloches or horticultural panes of glass held at the top with Rumsey clips can provide protection for the lower growing ones. This also produces earlier spring growth, either for cuttings or tea-making purposes. However, the best idea of all is the new invention from America of 'The Wall o' Water Plant Protector', which protects plants from freezing to well below minus 10 degrees. It is a 45cm-tall cylinder made of 6mm clear polythene plastic, the two layers of which are heat-sealed at 8cm intervals, forming pockets filled with water. The plants are warmed during the day by the plastic walls (there is adequate air circulation) and, meanwhile, the water pockets are being warmed ready to throw back the heat at the right time. Cheap, efficient and easily maintained, these provide the right balance for lemon verbena shrubs in their establishing years or struggling bay trees and rosemarys in a cold, damp situation.

chapter four

Routine or ritual?
The art of herbal drinks

The actual drinking of herbal teas can be clearly divided into two areas: that of daily functioning, where cups of herb tea must be drunk, with possible difficulties created by varying work situations or sheer lack of time; while perhaps in the evening or at weekends this herb tea drinking can resume a new role and provide a very pleasurable focal point of the day or night with all its attending ritual.

Routine and planning

Busy mothers, working folk, children at school and those at college all have a pretty tight schedule for at least ten hours of the day. This is the time when it is easy to say, 'Oh, I haven't got time to make a proper cup of tea', or, at worst, push money into a machine and retrieve some coloured water with a programmed taste. But with forethought this need not be the case.

The thermos flask has long been used to provide hot beverages for those away from home for the day and this, of course, can be used for herbal tea. Either some tea-bags can be popped into the flask which is then filled up with boiling water and a little honey, retrieving the bags when the first cup of tea is supped, or a large pot can be made and left to infuse and then poured into the flask, keeping one cup back from the pot for breakfast. Even if one doesn't move out of the home, the flask idea is often useful, although I rather like the excuse to down tools and fill my cup! Sometimes I use a very deep wicker sieve and pop a saucer over the mug to secure the aroma – unrefined but efficient!

If at work and one is lucky enough to have a structure where someone else makes the tea for you, then a tea-bag or tea-ball makes light work of refusing the standard tea or coffee – you can just ask for a cup of boiling water (have your own honey at hand). This applies if you are visiting friends with whom you must, of course, share the ritual of drinking something, or when lying in hospital where tea, coffee and hot chocolate are brought round at well-timed intervals. While for those going on holiday, when one is at the mercy of hotel staff or guest-house owners, this, again, is the time for a tea-bag or a tea-ball.

Tea-ball with scissor handle

Deep wicker sieve

Large 'meshed' tea-ball, these come in varying sizes.

Tea-ball with chain, which hooks onto edge of mug; unscrews in middle.

'Spice-infuser', ideal for adding a spice flavour to a 'standard tea-bag'; for instance, aniseed or cinnamon.

The 'zester' is an invaluable tool for removing the fresh rind of cirtrus fruits — yet leaving behind the pith — delicious in all teas.

There are many types of tea-balls and these are particularly useful when one has a special recipe which is not in a pre-packed tea-bag; it also allows more herb to be used, providing a 'stronger' cup of tea. Merely pack as much herb as you can into the tea-ball – about a tablespoonful – and leave in the mug to infuse for about 15 minutes.

Homemade tea-bags can be quickly made and produced out of a square of muslin. Place the dried herb in the middle and secure with an elastic band. All except the herb can be re-used after washing.

Solitary but civilised

There are many one-man ideas for brewing beverages and a most elegant one is the Chinese mug with the little matching lid (used by the Chinese for their fresh green teas). Having no infusion section to separate leaves from liquid, again either the tea-ball or tea-bag is best used with this. The peoples of Belgium, Hungary and Austria are used to their very pretty china mug infusers, complete with removable infuser section and lid. Then there are varying sizes of coffee infusers (one to six) which work on a compression idea. When the coffee pot has the powdered beans placed at the bottom, it is filled up with boiling water and the integral lid and infuser are secured, the latter gently pressed down to squash the coffee beans (or, in this case, the herb tea), leaving, after fifteen minutes or so, a beautifully infused liquid, separate from its beginnings.

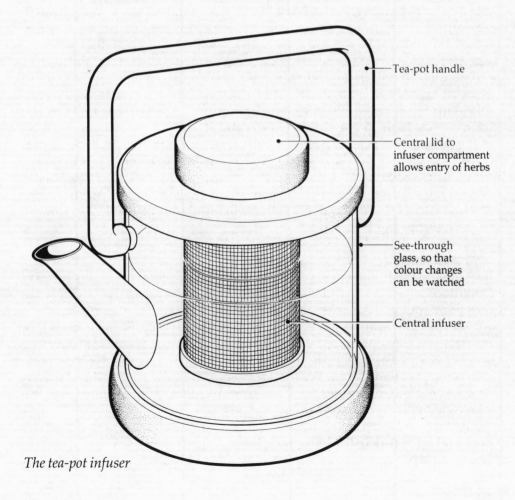

Tea-pot handle

Central lid to infuser compartment allows entry of herbs

See-through glass, so that colour changes can be watched

Central infuser

The tea-pot infuser

Leisure and ritual

We now climb to the top of the ladder for dealing with the infusion of a cup of herbal tea and this means gaining complete enjoyment and pleasure out of not just the flavour, colour, smell and taste of the herb tea, but of the art of making it.

The Japanese viewpoint

The basis of the Japanese ceremony came from China, as did the tea, but a lovely story triggered its whole beginnings. A dedicated Buddhist, wishing to serve Buddha with sleepless devotion for seven years, cut off his eyelids to keep awake. Throwing them away, they apparently sprouted two bushes – tea plants – the leaves of which would act as a stimulant for the sleepless devotee.

In the late fourteenth century the actual tea ceremony was born from those early beginnings, where the principles of the ceremony are those of frugality and restraint. The ceremony is performed for many reasons, either as one would expect, to pay homage to high-ranking officials, or for friends (usually five) or merely between a man and a woman. Both sexes can perform the ritual for each other, the essence being in the giving. It can mark an expression of love, that of conciliation and appeasement, and can represent the sharing of respect and admiration. The whole ritual can last from not less than an hour to four hours and at every stage of it appreciation of the surroundings is enjoyed, as with arranged flowers; all in the special tea house within a wooded section off a beautiful garden. It is a detailed, significant ceremony and training to perform it properly as a Tea Master takes many years. The Tea Master (like anybody who practises the ceremony to a less perfect degree) bears in mind four principles: harmony, respect, purity and tranquillity.

East and west

It sounds a little hollow to say that the drinking of herbal tea in this country should somehow lean towards the attitudes and essence of the Japanese tea ceremony, but just sample a fraction of what it is all about and it can be a very beautiful sensation. When sharing a meal with friends, my hope is that not only will the food be appetizing but beautifully presented and a feeling of giving and receiving should be experienced. I strive for complete enjoyment by all involved. We tend to accept and expect something special when going out to dinner, but tea drinking normally accompanies the television or disruption from other people.

Preparations and initial steps

The first step, therefore, to setting a standard for a more relaxed kind of herb tea drinking is to have a beautiful tea-set. For this, I occasionally use my great-grandmother's bone china one, but recently I wanted to give a very special birthday present so I bought a beautiful Chinese tea-pot, with a bamboo handle, matching tea bowls and a Chinese lacquered tray. This purchase came from the Chinese quarter in London's Gerrard Street, Soho.

Water quality

All that remains in order to make the tea is a kettle, some honey and a bamboo tea-strainer. While on the subject of kettles and therefore boiling water, I would like to comment on water quality. One only has to peer into the kettle to see the calcium residues which could form similar structures in the kidneys, being known more commonly as stones, plus the added chlorine, ammonia and, in some areas, fluoride. I have a very simple charcoal water filter to avoid this build up and this can be fitted over the tap; but there are many types of filters to choose from.

Tap water varies according to the area one lives in. For instance, London water is recycled many times and, among other things, contains residues of synthetic female hormones from the large number of women taking the pill, continuously recycled after urination; while in the country agricultural districts, chemical sprays permeate the water from the rain water supplies. Pure water rarely exists any more and avoiding some sort of water pollution is practically impossible.

Unlike the Japanese tea ceremony, I prepare the pot and fill it with water in the kitchen and bring the infusing pot complete with bowls to wherever we have chosen to drink the tea; in winter it would probably be the sitting room, but in summer any number of intimate areas like those described in Chapter three could be used.

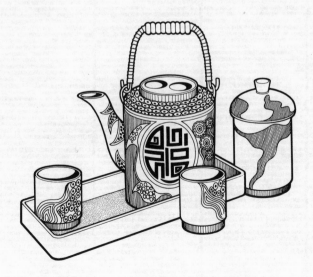

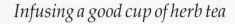

Infusing a good cup of herb tea

Having assembled the appropriate equipment, we are now faced with using it correctly. Like any good cup of tea, the first step is to warm the pot. A text book quantity of herbal tea is 25g to half a litre of water, but I always say a dessertspoon to tablespoon for a pint tea-pot. Then pour on the boiling water and swiftly replace the lid to stop the herbs' essential oils evaporating. For the tea to be at a suitable drinking temperature and also so that the tea has sufficiently infused and imparted to the water all its valuable qualities, it should be left for 15 minutes. Halfway through this time, one can stir the water, immediately replacing the lid with a final stir before serving. I like to use a bamboo tea-strainer as plastic or aluminium are unsympathetic and the latter can impart a bad taste.

Enhancing additions

The mixture of herbs used for the tisane will dictate its natural sweetness, bitterness, warmth or coldness (to be discussed in Chapter five) and, therefore, will affect the various embellishments or additions one may or may not wish to add. If a lemony-flavoured tea has been mixed, then it might be nice to enforce the flavour with a slice of lemon, while a spicy tea on a cold day might be further 'heated' by adding freshly-grated ginger – but more detail on flavour balancing will appear in Chapter five.

If sweetness is desired then we do not ever suggest using sugar (it strips calcium from the system and poisons the bloodstream, to name but two of its vices), rather honey is always recommended. Another source of natural sweetness is fructose, obtained at a price, from fresh fruit and available in most health food stores. Malted barley is not only a good natural sweetener, but is also rich in vitamin B. Its texture is similar to that of honey and it is dark brown in colour.

Honey

Honey is really a complete food and very easily digested, consisting almost entirely of pure glucose and levulose, as well as other substances necessary for cell, tissue and normal organ functioning. Beet and cane sugar have to undergo changes in order to be absorbed, being broken down into glucose and levulose by the digestive juices, then into the bloodstream and finally carried to the liver – all of which is a strain on the system.

Honey contains many enzymes, some of them important for the conversion of cane sugar. Other highly important constituents of honey are its mineral content, such as calcium, phosphorus, sulphur, sodium, potassium, magnesium, iron, chlorine and iodine salts. Some honeys – polyfloral and buckwheat – even contain manganese, silicon, aluminium, boron, chromium, copper, lithium, nickel, zinc and osmium. All mineral salts are highly important to an efficiently working body.

In addition, honey contains some organic acids, all of which are substances which increase the activity of the body, like malic, citric and oxalic acid. (This factor can be easily proven by using it as a growth inducer when taking plant cuttings.) Although containing natural acids, this must not be confused with the fact that honey is basically an alkaline food and vital, therefore, in acid-neutralising and the alkaline balance of the body, which normally tends to be overbalanced in the acidity direction. This factor ties in with its mineral content, as the higher the mineral content the higher the alkaline value. This can be clearly worked out when buying honeys as the darker coloured ones are highest in mineral content, although it is always the very pale, almost translucent ones which win the prizes! The nutritive and therapeutic qualities of honey are further enhanced by its excellent vitamin content which are vitamins B_2, B_6, H, K, C, among others. The vitamin content of the honey is dependent on the quality of pollen within it and if this is ever filtered out, then all vitamins are lost.

All honey acts as a disinfectant, having strong anti-bacterial and antimycotic properties (the latter preventing the growth of moulds and fungi). It is a great healer of wounds, wonderful for a host of upper respiratory diseases including the common cold, beneficial for heart diseases (improvement of the cardiac muscles are helped by honey), also for gastric and intestinal diseases – generally improving the digestive system and assimilation of food. The liver and its filtering function is aided by honey, while the nervous system is indebted to the natural glucose and its other components. It is a general help to skin diseases, eye diseases and for post-operative care, combining nutrition and healing factors. The list is endless and only a smattering of the curative, rejuvenative properties of honey have been mentioned, however enough, I hope, to persuade any who were doubtful that the only sweet accompaniment is *honey*.

Different honeys: native, imported, polyfloral, singles

The question in your minds might now be which honey to buy? The best honey of all is that which your own bees have produced, preferably eaten off the comb during summer. Flora of your own vicinity (the flight path of the bees being two to three miles) is the most beneficial to you and can even help in immunising the body against pollen irritation in cases of hayfever. Our family has two hives, providing 500–750g of honey a week – we find this just about enough to cover our yearly needs.

I dislike being forced to buy honey from shops for many reasons. If not using my own honey, I buy from a known, medium-sized apiary, where good bee-keeping and honey processing is carried out. Indiscrimination about whether the bees have fed on chemically sprayed fields, plus the fact that the bees may have been entirely fed on cane or beet sugar without going near a plant and its pollen, warns me away from supermarkets. Certainly, in this country, with our close-knit agricultural system, even a country garden free from chemical spraying may lead into a sprayed field as part of the flight path of the bees. So, having said that native honey is the best, unless you are really sure of the source, a honey like Spanish rosemary, taken from the mountain sides of Spain where the peasants do not have the money for chemical sprays, might be a good choice. Others include Mexican organic honey and Hungarian acacia honey.

However, having said that, overseas' honey may avoid chemical sprays, but much overseas' honey is 'heated' to kill off a bee disease (the disease is not prevalent in this country and, therefore, not heated for those reasons), and this also kills off many of its medicinal properties. Again, the honey is shipped in large containers where it sets and is, therefore, sometimes heated (instead of slowly warmed) to move it from these containers to the honey jars.

How much honey?

Having now chosen your honey, preferably from a known, local source, the question is how much honey is it wise or beneficial to consume? As with anything, balance is the key note (anything excessive is bad, even if it is *good*!). So as a guideline, one jar per healthy adult over a period of two weeks would be a suitable intake. However, honey will make you nauseous if you over-indulge – this is the body's way of telling you about your excesses! Take care also that children and infants also gain a balanced intake, suitable for their body weight.

Taste and particular medicinal qualities

Every honey not only contains the therapeutic qualities previously mentioned but each has the particular medicinal quality of the plant or plants a bee has fed upon. For instance, rosemary honey is highly antiseptic and I particularly enjoy its flavour as it is a naturally bitter herb and, softened with the sweetness, the result is a rather savoury honey. Buckwheat honey ranks high on my list of excellent honeys, because it is very dark and therefore high in mineral salts, but added to this is the fact that buckwheat herb is specifically good for strengthening arteries and, therefore, ideal for any degenerative diseases. Alfalfa honey would be an almost untouchable complete vitamin source as alfalfa is a multiple vitamin plant anyway. While clover honey would be excellent involved in a tisane specifically designed for blood purification and tonic properties as red clover itself is a blood purifer.

If you are buying honey from a wholefood or health food store, with all the choice at your fingertips, then it might be nice to have a selection, making an evaluation on matching not only a harmonising tasting honey but also one that will enhance the brew medicinally. If, like myself, you have your own source then this is, of course, the finest and I know that my own honey is a medicine cabinet in itself as my bees feed on thyme, comfrey, yarrow, balm, betony, wormwood, rosemary, and all the many hundreds of species beyond these; and with a taste to match their efforts – pure nectar of the gods!

Incidentally, if I or anybody ever gets stung by my own bees, the prescription is to eat spoonfuls of their own produce to counteract the effects and any shock which may have been encountered.

Masking a medicinal flavour

Occasionally a mixture of herbs is put together for purely medicinal reasons and the taste may not be all that pleasant, although I try and make anything I formulate, for whatever purpose, a pleasurable experience. I'm sure it is for this very reason that herbal teas have, in the past (and with some blends, still do), 'a grin and bear it' association.

I recently came across a lovely extract from the memoirs of my Welsh great-great grandfather, William Davies (1819–1904). Aged 70 years old, he wrote:

> *'During my stay at Mold [north Wales], I laid myself out for drinking a large quantity of herb teas which my mother used to send me in several gallons at a time and I have no doubt but that it did me a lot of good.'*

These were indeed days of temperance and chapel! Nowadays, attitudes have changed a great deal and certainly children, if not adults included, are not expected to drink odd tasting drinks for their own good. One formula that springs to mind is my 'Calcium tea', which is vital for young, growing bones, teeth and nervous system. Not particularly palatable, I disguise the taste with apple juice concentrate. Naturally sweet from the apples, this addition does not even require honey and, as a concentrate, can easily be diluted with the tea infusion. Many exciting concentrates made from fresh fruits are available from wholefood shops, like grape juices (red and black) and blackcurrant juice. These are *not* to be confused with 'squashes' however, which are nothing more than sugary, chemical concoctions, responsible for problems like hyperactive children and rotting teeth.

Root teas

The generally accepted formula for a herbal tea is made up of leaves, flowers and buds, in other words, all the parts of the plant which are tender and easily infused in water. However, I frequently add roots and stalks which are obviously of a much tougher nature, but if one allows 15 minutes for infusion time, then certainly the finely chopped roots or rhizomes go a long way to rendering up their valuable qualities.

To extract every inch of goodness from roots, rhizomes or stalks, there is a method called 'a decoction', which is a 20-minute simmer in a double saucepan. The end result is usually a thick, dark, sticky liquid which is similarly strong tasting. This can be added to an infusion of the aerial parts of the plant, but this arduous way of making tea would really only be reserved for purely medicinal purposes and might, at the end of it, need some concentrated fruit juices added due to the very strong flavour.

Many root teas taste delightful and the old American drink, sarsaparilla, was made on the lines of a decoction, while its pleasant taste was known by most of Victorian Britain. Burdock and dandelion was, and still is, a time-old combination and not just due to its undeniably excellent tonic properties – it does have a very pleasant and intriguing flavour.

Herb coffee

Herb coffees are generally accepted as being mostly 'roots' that have been roasted, hence the coffee association with its roasted beans. It has its advantages also, especially for people who do hanker after a roasted and rather bitter flavour, like that of coffee, and who have given up or are trying to abstain from coffee drinking. The pre-chopped roots, rhizomes, bark or stalks can be easily bought, like comfrey, marshmallow, dandelion, burdock and sarsaparilla roots, or wild cherry bark and liquorice rhizome. These should then be laid on a baking sheet so that they will roast evenly, in a slow oven (250°F, 130°C) for an hour or two (depending on the size of the herb part) until crisp. This should then be left to cool and used as it is, or it can be ground in a coffee grinder in order to extract more flavour. However, it does store better if left unground, so only grind to your particular needs at a time. I do have some exciting recipes for roasted herb coffee, but these will be aired in the last chapter.

Brewing the roasted herb

The techniques for making a cup of roasted root tea is exactly the same as for coffee, i.e. either with a percolator or the compression pot earlier described, or simply in the 'farmer's style', which is to pour boiling water on to the grounds and leave it to brew for 20 minutes before straining and re-heating. Again, I often like to mix my roasted parts of the herbal tea, combining, say, roasted rhizome with buds and flowers (recipes, Chapter five) and, therefore, infusing all together.

Preserving herbs for year-round drinking

Enjoyment of natural teas and coffee is, as I have said earlier, a four-seasons activity and generally one would find it convenient to buy most of the ingredients for the teas, unless one has a garden and can grow the easier ones. Even so, harvesting, preparing and drying is quite an art in itself, especially for roots and rhizomes. Therefore, unless you are familiar with this side of things, use them fresh during the summer and purchase in winter. Having said that I will just simply outline some harvesting and storage ideas for the adventurous and keen.

How to harvest

Choose a warm, sunny day, after the dew has dried but before the fierce sun has arrived. Pick only those plant parts not deformed or damaged by insects, placing in a basket or container that can breathe – not plastic. Never over-pick and always leave a plant looking as if no one has been near it.

If making fresh teas at this point, the next procedure is simple – just crush the flower or foliage so that its flavour can escape more easily into the hot water, using double the quantity of fresh herbs as you would dried. Otherwise, the plant material should be laid on muslin or thin cotton on a cake rack, or hung in small bunches, which can then be hung from beams, hooks, or a homemade line, in order to dry. The herbs on the rack can then be placed in an airing cupboard or on window-sills, but with the curtains drawn – as direct sunlight strips the essential oils and the tea will initially lose most of its flavour.

Drying should take one to three days (and should be at a temperature of no higher than 90°F, 65°C), depending on the weather – any longer than this and it is likely that they will become mouldy and spoil. They should be brittle and shrivelled if properly dry, although still retaining their colour. A good test for dryness is to put a sample in a jam jar and place it in the sunshine, if water droplets appear on the lid, then the moisture content is still too high and the drying process must continue.

Partially-dried leaves must not be used for tea because certain species are toxic at this twilight stage, when their chemistry changes in very subtle ways; the same plant being quite safe either fresh or totally dry.

Storage

Just as during the drying process of the herb, the storage must continue to be out of direct sunlight. For this, dark jars with airtight stoppers are ideal but plain, clear jam jars are fine, although best stored themselves in a cupboard. The leaves, flowers and buds should be stored as whole as possible to retain their potency, crushing only for making the tea. Most important now is to label the jars to avoid confusion.

You will notice that I have only described the collection of the aerial parts of the herb. This is because, as I previously mentioned, roots, rhizomes and barks are hard to prepare properly and require some expertise, sometimes needing a seven-year period of delay before using the part required – so this is best left to skilled hands and purchased on need. Beyond anything else, digging up roots does mean the destruction of the plant, unlike taking a few leaves and flowers.

chapter five

Understanding herbs

No formal training can create a 'true' wholistic herbalist. Imagination and intuition must work together. The latter can only develop with time and practice, using the senses of smell, touch and taste. Growing plants and watching them grow is the first step to encouraging an intuitive awareness of herbs. This chapter deals with dried herbs. Again new sensory and intuitive perception is required due to the changes that have taken place in the herb from its fresh and vital form to its dried state.

Before one can venture into the realms of blending and formulating personal recipes it is important to become familiar with the flavour of each herb. The last chapter outlined how to prepare and enjoy herb teas and touched on drying one's own herbs for this purpose, but equally vital is the need to be familiar with the quality of herbs which you are to drink.

Quality first

A great many shops, ranging from your local supermarket to delicatessen, from gift shop to whole food shop, now all sell a reasonably good range of herbs, while others specialise in more medicinal ones. For this reason it is now possible to be more choosy about your intended purchase.

Quality is most readily detected by the colour and, secondly, smell of herbs, if not in sealed bags. Sometimes the herbs have been displayed in direct sunlight with a slow turnover of stock, producing a dull, tired specimen, lacking in flavour and potency. It is hard at first to become instantly knowledgeable about what colour all herbs should be in their freshly dried state. I always suggest using parsley as a test as, dried, it should be a bright mid-green; very often it is rather pale and slightly grey-brown. Parsley is one of the herb top-sellers, so if this is tired-looking it is likely that the rest of the herb range of that particular shop will be, too.

If you ever find a good source of dried herbs it is always wise to stick to it. This may mean using mail order as such companies sometimes miss out some of the stages of smaller shops and reach the consumer much faster. Likewise, large turnover shops have a more direct link with the wholesalers, so it means detective work on your own part – beyond harvesting your own!

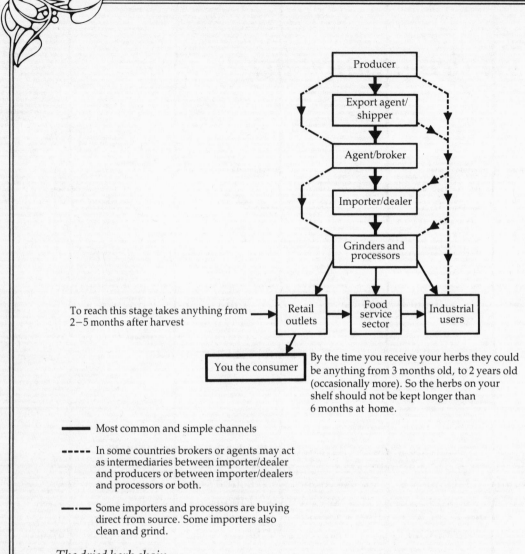

To reach this stage takes anything from 2–5 months after harvest

By the time you receive your herbs they could be anything from 3 months old, to 2 years old (occasionally more). So the herbs on your shelf should not be kept longer than 6 months at home.

——— Most common and simple channels

- - - - In some countries brokers or agents may act as intermediaries between importer/dealer and producers or between importer/dealers and processors or both.

—·— Some importers and processors are buying direct from source. Some importers also clean and grind.

The dried herb chain

Individual herb flavours, their colour and smell

This is indeed a daunting task and one where there are really no short cuts. The first job is, of course, to buy in all the herbs. I suggest buying just 25g of each until you have decided upon a short list, and for your help I have devised a chart listing the herbs discussed in Chapter two. Those very commonly used have been given an asterisk. Secondly, for those who have perhaps just a few of the fresh specimens in their gardens, then this experiment should take place during summer in order to compare the dried herb next to the fresh.

When ordering the herbs, you must be careful to specify that you do not wish them powdered – they should be rubbed or chopped. Some herbs are virtually only available in the powdered form, though this is generally the minority. Incidentally, powdered herbs are a different colour from their chopped counterpart and obviously have a far shorter shelf life.

Having already discussed the visual appearance of each herb in Chapter two, I am not repeating the description but centring on the dried specimen from which to make your own fresh evaluations for contrast. There is a column for 'taste' and this has been taken as the taste of the dried plant when infused in boiling water for 15 minutes. If your own findings are measurably lower than my own description then it is obvious that the dried herbs you have are of inferior quality. On the chart, the column for smell is based on the dried, non-infused specimen, as is the colour of the dried plant. This is a very quick way to identify quality before going to the trouble of making a cup of tea!

Being able to identify dried plants without the aid of a label is really most important but especially if it's one's own commercial business. This is because, very occasionally, mistakes do occur and remain unfound by the normally very stringent series of checks that have to be made; in this case it is most important to detect a possibly dangerous error of contamination – for instance, a toxic plant being harvested alongside the non-toxic.

Plant name	Parts of plant used	Colour (dry)	Taste (infused)	Smell (dry)
Agrimony	Leaf and stem	Mid-green	Bland and grass-like	New-mown hay smell
Alfalfa	Foliage	Dark green and flecked blue-white, if with its flowers	Bland, but fresh	Nondescript but fresh smell
Allspice	Berry	Pale brown, flecked dark	Strong, spicy hints of clove and nutmeg. Warming	Quite strong, spicy aroma
Aloe vera	Stalks, often the expressed juice	Bright green leaves, or clear pale green liquid	Pleasant, slightly sweet; mucilaginous, sticky	No particular smell

Plant name	Parts of plant used	Colour (dry)	Taste (infused)	Smell (dry)
Anise	Star-shaped seed-coat with seeds	Dark brown husk with shiny polished seed-coat	Aniseed taste, very pungent. Hot and warming	Very strong aniseed flavour
Balm, Lemon	Flower bud, leaf and stem	Bright green; white flecks of chopped stalk	Pleasant, lemony flavour, but gentle. Cooling	Lemon smell, not as strong as lemon verbena
Bergamot	Flower, leaf and stem	Mid-green; red flecks of flowers	Perfumed taste, slightly sweet. Lovely flavour	Highly scented
Betony, Wood	Leaf and stem	Mid-green; white flecks of cut stem	Reasonably bland	Sweet, grass-like smell
Blessed thistle	Leaf and stem	Pale green; white flecks	Blandish taste	No particular smell, but fresh
Borage	Flower, leaf and stem	Blue flecks of flowers; dark bottle green leaf colour	Full-flavoured. Cooling	Sweet and fresh
Buckwheat	Leaves	Dark green	Blandish, but pleasant	Bland
Burdock	Root	Pale brown; flecked white	Strong pleasant taste, faintly liquorice-like. Warming	Slightly sweet, with faint liquorice smell
Caraway	Seed	Dark brown	Incredibly strong caraway flavour. Positive, pleasant taste	Smells strong and pungent

Plant name	Parts of plant used	Colour (dry)	Taste (infused)	Smell (dry)
Catnip	Leaf and stem	Pale green; flecked white	Pretty bland, but pleasant	Faintly sweet
Cayenne	Fruit	Mid-rosy, orange (not as pale as paprika, less dark than chilli)	Hot and burning. Very positive	Spicy, full-flavoured. Irritant to the nose
Centaury	Leaf and stem	Mid-green; flecked white	Bland and gentle	Hay-like
Chamomile	Flowers	Golden yellow and white	Sweet, pleasant taste. Slightly warming. SHOULD NOT BE INFUSED FOR 15 MINS. EVEN A SINGLE TEA 5–7 MINS CAN PRODUCE NAUSEA.	Strong, sweetish smell, sometimes a little sickly
Cherry tree	Bark	Brown-red outer shiny bark with very pale inner bark	Blandish, pleasant, 'twiggy' flavour	Smells just as it is, trees and twigs, etc.
Chickweed	Whole, cropped herb	Bright, bottle green	Blandish, quite pleasant	Fresh, grassy smell
Cinnamon	Inner bark of shoots	Pale brown with red hints	Warm, pungent flavour	Pungent smell released further on breaking the stick

Plant name	Parts of plant used	Colour (dry)	Taste (infused)	Smell (dry)
Clover, Red	Flowers, leaves and stem	Pale red flecks of flowers. Mid-green leaf and stalk colour	Sweetish, very pleasant	Light, gentle smell
Coltsfoot	Leaves	Soft to handle. Mid sage-green and woolly white parts	Blandish taste with different aftertaste, not unpleasant	Slightly acrid smell
Comfrey	Leaves	Dark green	Strongish taste, quite pleasant, nondescript. Leaves tongue furry	Strongish, hay-like smell
	Root	Mid to dark brown	Quite a positive flavour, but nondescript	Strongish, but no particular smell
Coriander	Seeds, also leaves and stalks	Seeds are palish brown-grey; leaves, bright green	Seeds are spicy and aromatic; leaves, very pungent and strong	Seeds smell spicy and aromatic; leaves, pungent and strong
Dandelion	Root (leaves used fresh)	Dark brown and white	Pleasant, sweetish flavour	Sweetish smell
Devil's claw	Chopped root for teas	Yellow/white	Rather bitter, though not excessively so (seeds are bitter)	Strongish, interesting smell
Dill	Seed (leaves used fresh)	Beige to mid-brown	Dill flavour! Similar to aniseed	Strong, sweet flavour, pungent

Plant name	Parts of plant used	Colour (dry)	Taste (infused)	Smell (dry)
Dock, Yellow	Root	Warm brown-yellow	Sweetish, pleasant flavour	No particular smell
Echinacea	Root	Mid to dark brown	Nondescript flavour, but faintly bitter	No particular smell
Elderflower	Flowers	Primrose yellow	Fruity sweet, very pleasant flavour	Fruity, sweet smell
Eyebright	Stem, flower and leaves	Greenish brown, but mostly mid-green	Blandish, but pleasant taste	Hay-like
Fennel	Leaves and stem	Mid-green, flecked white from stalks	Dill-like flavour, but less strong. Lovely	Sweet, sharp smell
Ginger	Root (should be used fresh if possible, grated) Flakes	When fresh, it is yellow-brown, tinged green. When dried, it is creamy-yellow	When fresh, tastes very strong and hot. When dried, it loses its heat and moisture and quite a bit of its flavour and bite. Extremely good flavour	Smells 'gingery' and very alive when fresh. When dried it hardly smells at all
Ginseng	Root	Browny-yellow, depending on the species	A reasonably passive taste. Slightly warming	An interesting smell, but almost indescribable
Golden rod	Flowers, leaves and stalk	Darkish green and white flecks of the stalks; yellow	Pleasant, blandish flavour	Interesting, but not notable smell

Plant name	Parts of plant used	Colour (dry)	Taste (infused)	Smell (dry)
		and white flower heads		
Hawthorn	Berries and flowers	Scarlet berries; white, pink or red flowers	Berries, slightly bitter; flowers, quite sweet	No particular smell
Hibiscus	Flowers	Dark maroon-red	Strong delightful flavour! Fresh, sweet and very distinctive	Sweet, attractive smell
Hops	Flowers	Very pale green; sticky to touch	Slightly bitter flavour, though not as strong as varieties used in brewing beer	Strong, slightly bitter smell
Horehound, White	Leaves and stalk	Whitish to mid-green; woolly	Bland	A musky smell, which disappears the longer it is kept
Horsetail	Fleshy, aerial stems	Mid-sage-green	Blandish flavour	Nondescript smell
Kelp	Whole, chopped herb	Dark green and brown	Salty and seaweedy	Salty and seaweedy
Lavender	Buds and flowers	Dark blue tips, generally mid-blue-lilac with green bases	Slightly bitter-sweet taste, very strong	Sweet, highly aromatic smell; should be very strong
Lemon tree	Fruit	Lemon-yellow!	Lemon-flavoured!	Lemon smell!
	The fresh fruit is always advised; dried is available but not recommended			

Plant name	Parts of plant used	Colour (dry)	Taste (infused)	Smell (dry)
Linden or Lime tree	Flowers, as fresh as possible. Stale flowers can become slightly toxic	Greeny/cream	Sweet and quite strong	Sweet and flowery
Liquorice	Rhizomes and root	Outer thin bark is dark brown, while inner thick bark is white	Liquorice taste is strong and known by most. Warming flavour, very pleasant	Liquorice smell familiar to most. Bitter-sweet
Marigold	Petals	Golden, deep orange	Soft to the mouth, a little sweet; quite pleasant with a salty aftertaste	Nondescript, a little sweet
Marjoram	Leaves and stalks	Mid-green	A little bitter and antiseptic in flavour	Pungent, sweet-bitter smell
Marshmallow	Leaves	Soft to handle. Mid-sage-green and woolly white parts; visually very similar to Coltsfoot	Strong taste, a little unpleasant. Needs to be disguised. Soft texture to the tongue	Slightly 'foul' smell, though not unpleasant
Meadow-sweet	Leaves and stalk	Darkish green, woolly-looking leaves; pale green stalks	Very pleasant, light, sweetish flavour	A heady, sweetish smell
Mints	All have very distinct yet very similar flavours and smells			
Spearmint	Leaves and stalk	Dark green	Very strong flavour; warming in cold weather, cooling in hot	A strong smell, reminiscent of chewing gum!

63

Plant name	Parts of plant used	Colour (dry)	Taste (infused)	Smell (dry)
Peppermint	Leaves and stalk	Lighter green than spearmint, but still dark. More stalk usually	Very strong flavour. Warming qualities in cold weather, cooling in hot	A strong smell, usually associated with culinary products e.g. sweets, rock, etc
Pennyroyal	Flowers, leaves and stalk	Fresh mid-green	Strong flavour	Fresh, sweet and strong
Motherwort	Leaves and stalk	Mid-green	Blandish taste	Nondescript smell
Mullein, Great	Leaves	Mid to dark green; soft and fluffy to handle	Blandish flavour, quite pleasant	Non-describable, vaguely sweet
Nettles	Leaves and stalk	Dark green; whitish bits of stalks	Strongish flavour of no particular character	Slightly foul odour, though not unpleasant
Parsley	Leaves	Bright, vivid green	Bland taste	Hay-like, slightly bitter
Plantain	Leaves	Pale green	Bland taste	Nondescript smell
Poke root	Root	Mid-brown with pink tinges	Not too pleasant	Strongish
Raspberry, Red	Leaves	Darkish green; soft to handle	Bitter, slightly unpleasant; rather strong	Nondescript smell
Rosehip	Hips or fruit (with seed)	Orange-red; paler tiny seeds	Rather sharp with a hint of sweet. Very pleasant to taste	Vaguely sweet, blandish smell

Plant name	Parts of plant used	Colour (dry)	Taste (infused)	Smell (dry)
Rosemary	Leaves	Mid-green on underside; dark green on top	Bitter flavour, strong but not unpleasant	Bitter, interesting smell, rather antiseptic
Sage	Leaves	Mid-pale green	Strong, bitter flavour	Bitter, strong smell, antiseptic
St John's wort	Flowers, leaf and stalk	Flowers, yellow-ochre; otherwise green, brown and beige	Rather clean, pleasant flavour	Fresh, sweetish smell
Sarsaparilla, Jamaican	Root	Pale brown and beige	Flavour needs long infusion, i.e. 'decoction' in order to extract true flavour	Bland smell
Sassafras	Root and bark	Dark brown	Pleasant, rounded, slightly spicy flavour	No particular smell until infused
Scullcap, Virginian	Leaf and stalk	Pale green with white stem and stalk pieces	Blandish taste but pretty pleasant	Slightly sweet, but nothing interesting
Thyme	Leaves (rubbed)	Pale green	Strong, bitter-sweet flavour	Sweet, savoury smell, very pleasant
Verbena, Lemon	Leaves	Fresh mid-green	Strong lemon flavour, but not 'citrus lemon' taste	Strong lemon smell, but again not the smell of 'citrus lemon'

Plant name	Parts of plant used	Colour (dry)	Taste (infused)	Smell (dry)
Vervain, Blue	Leaves and stalk	Mid-dark green	Tastes a little like green China tea	Smells similar to China tea
Yarrow	Flowers, leaves and stalk	Dirty, pale yellow	Rather bitter taste. Should never be in large proportions	Slightly acrid smell

Scent and flavour of essential oils

These will occasionally be added to the tea recipes, so let us explore their background. First of all, what is an essential oil? The answer is often confusing, especially as lots of plants are aromatic – either the whole plant, or part of it – and these odours are not all due to essential oils.

Essential oils are found in minute cell sacs in sections of the plant like their buds, petals and leaves and sometimes their stems, barks, woods, rhizomes, roots, fruit and seeds. The essential oils can either be released and liberated by the heat of the sun or by crushing the leaf or just by brushing past the plant. All these actions rupture the essential oil cells. Some plants smell very strong, even without the help of strong sun or crushing, while others need hard bruising to impart their lovely perfumes. Not all essential oils are beautiful, however; some can be most unpleasant or just rather nauseous. Their role in the plant is not just to delight or disgust human beings but to attract pollinating insects and keep pests and parasites at bay; they may also be the waste product or 'excretion' of other life processes within the plant.

One of the most colourful examples of a plant which releases its oil on sunny days without the need for any other assistance is white dittany; this plant was very likely the 'burning bush' in the Bible. This lemon-scented plant has millions of oil-producing glands and these volatile oils escape in the form of a flammable vapour and may not even need a match to ignite them – spontaneous combustion could well have performed the apparent miracle in the Bible! The plant, interestingly enough, is left intact.

The story behind essential oils
Essential oils are extracted from the plant either by expression, distillation or extraction. These processes are fairly complicated and if you have further

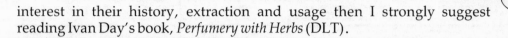

interest in their history, extraction and usage then I strongly suggest reading Ivan Day's book, *Perfumery with Herbs* (DLT).

Their use

For using with herbal teas, for enhancing flavour or returning the essential oils sometimes lost in the drying process of the plant, I have set out a table for easy reference. I have only mentioned reasonably easy to obtain oils and ones which are truly useful and safe. For instance, there is probably little point in using aniseed oil in a tea as aniseed itself is so strong.

The other reason for using essential oils as part of a formula is for their medicinal value, and where perhaps the actual plant itself might be left out, its essential oil can be added producing greater potency and strength. It is important to know about essential oils – very often they smell nothing like the plant they have come from as they are so concentrated. However, sensitively used in minute quantities and mixed into dried herbs, they not only bring added vitality to the herbs but suddenly take on their plant scent once again. But take note: some essential oils are incredibly strong in their concentrated state and dealing with them can either be a lovely experience or really rather unpleasant. For instance, I find neat peppermint oil gives me a headache and so when I am mixing it into teas I use a muslin nose and mouth mask.

Oil	Part of plant used	Smell and flavour	Strength and usage
Chamomile, Blue	Flowers	Fragrant, sweet and quite strong, slightly apple-scented	Very strong. Use sparingly as its medicinal action is potent and must be balanced carefully, i.e. half pipette drop to 100–125g tea
Citron	Fruit rind	Citrus, lemon-like and fresh	Reasonably strong
Citronella	Leaves of winter's grass	Lemon-like, though rather oily and cloying	Rather strong, use sparingly
Clove	Dried, immature flowers of clove	Strongly spicy	Very strong, useful for disguising flavours

Oil	Part of plant used	Smell and flavour	Strength and usage
Lavender	Flowers	Very strong, not resembling lavender plant at all, rather piercing	Use very sparingly
Lemon verbena, Spanish	Leaves, buds and flowers	Lemon-like	Fairly strong
Monarda	Leaves and flowers of bergamot (*monarda didyma*). NB: not to be confused with bergamot orange oil	Rather similar to lavender, i.e. sharpish	Strong, use sparingly
Orange	Peel of bitter orange	Fresh orange scent	Fairly strong
Orange, Jaffa	From the Jaffa orange	Sweet and strong orange scent	Use liberally as very cheap and doesn't hold smell as well as most
Peppermint	Flowering tops of peppermint	Minty and fresh, very strong and heady	Use sparingly
Pine	From the needles and cones of the pine tree	Very strong, pine-like scent, bitter flavour	Use very sparingly in conjunction with another oil
Rose, Otto	Petals of the damask rose	Sweet and heavy, rose essence can be cloying	Rather persistent, so use sparingly
Rose, Geranium	Geranium plant oil and fresh rose petals distilled together	Very rose-like	Strongish

Note: Rose oils are best added extremely sparingly, just a hint should be the result

Oil	Part of plant used	Smell and flavour	Strength and usage
Rosemary	Flowers and leaf tops	Very strong smell, does not resemble rosemary. Medicinal, camphorus smell and taste	Use sparingly
Sage	Leaves and flowers	Strong and camphorus, rather antiseptic in smell. Medicinal in flavour	Strong
Spearmint	Leaves and flowers	Rather sweet spearmint flavour. Smell, fresh	Use sparingly, is persistent like all mint oils
Thyme	Leaves and flowers	Strong, medicinal smell and flavour	Use sparingly

Note: Remember that roughly seven million flower heads go to make a drop of essential oil.

The more medicinal oils

Beyond lavender, sage, rosemary and thyme, all the herb essential oils here have pleasant, distinctive flavours and tastes. The above can also be pleasant, especially lavender, but they are essentially medicinal and their powers for averting illness and disease are well-known.

There is a famous plague story set in the fourteenth century: told frequently and in many different ways the rough outline remains pretty much the same. It is that some grave robbers were found with vast amounts of gold, jewels and collected wealth. The query was, how these robbers (looting the graves of the rich who had died from the highly infectious plague) could still be alive. In return for their lives they confessed to rubbing the leaves of thyme, rosemary, sage and lavender over their bodies each morning. The essential oils of these highly antiseptic, antibiotic plants gave them their protection. It became known as the 'Four Thieves Mixture' and was often mixed with vinegar. Later on in France, in the perfume factories, the girls handling essential oil of lavender were found to escape from various lethal diseases like typhoid.

So the addition of these essential oils in herbal teas will be minor and sensitive, used really only where their medicinal value is very much favoured. Chamomile oil should also be shown respect, as it is a strongly acting herb even in its fresh or dried plant form.

Examples will be shown in Chapter six.

Techniques for balancing flavours

One of the first requirements for this activity is an ability to distinguish clearly by smell and taste. Whether you are approaching this on a very simple kitchen basis or taking the subject more seriously, the methods of evaluation remain the same. It must also be remembered that there is no substitute for the personal experience of constant mixing and tasting. These skills develop with time, until a point is reached where a taste is conjured up merely by mentally mixing together specific herbs.

The organs of sensation become overburdened very quickly with repeated stimulation so it is, therefore, best to carry out experiments over a period of days, preferably first thing in the morning while the palate is untainted by other flavours and odours. Otherwise, one should also feel healthy – a trace of a hangover is an obvious non-starter or a cold would stall any experiments, although a drink of peppermint, yarrow and elderflower tea would speed the recovery from this set-back! Ideally, one should have a small bowl for each herb and these should all be clearly labelled, much in the same way as I discussed trying to learn the smells of each dried herb at the beginning of this chapter.

One of the prime objectives is to create something pleasant to drink and so we are really aiming for this, rather than aiding the body in some way. The more medicinal side of things will be discussed in Chapter six, covering the wholistic approach, incorporating herbs not necessarily aimed at being flavoursome.

Keeping records

The method of quantity/proportions measurement is never easy, as the method by which the individual herb has been prepared can alter the procedure greatly, i.e. fresh or dried, chopped, rubbed, powdered. For instance, a fresh herb is roughly three times the amount of its dried counterpart, while rosehips, fresh or chopped dry, are infinitely less in quantity compared to the weight than, say, of elderflower – gramme for gramme. You must establish a consistent method of measurement so the record of the proportions for future use can be maintained. The keeping of accurate records cannot be over emphasised as memories often play tricks.

On the label of each bowl not only should the name of the plant appear, but also the age of the plant, i.e. the year and, if possible, the month of collection. Life is made very easy by having a pair of accurate scales that weigh small amounts in grammes. One should also have one or two large mixing bowls with a wooden spoon. The scene would seem to be set for making a cake and, in fact, the kitchen is probably the most appropriate place for this exercise.

The methods and order of balancing flavours for the making of herb teas will vary according to the individual. Some will wish to weigh, mix and taste, while others will mix in pinches, taste and then guess at the weight to finally match tastes. The best method is the one where personal achievement is met with enjoyment and success! My own method is probably a mixture of the two mentioned above. With a note book and pen at hand, I plunge in, starting with the herbs I know to have weak flavours first (individual flavours previously discussed) and I work in pinches. For example, I might start with a pinch of chamomile and a pinch of hibiscus; my note book now has two entries. Depending on the outcome of the marriage of these two tastes, we can continue, perhaps adding a small pinch of spearmint, tasting again. We have now a combination of three plants. By our side we will have a drink made of the combination of two and a combination of three. This allows us to taste both, moving backwards and forwards from one to another, for the first time, perhaps, gaining insight into the flavour changes due to blending. One will be distinctly different from the other. At this point, some personal method of distinguishing this difference must be made as one must be clear as to whether the flavour has improved or deteriorated; has become more passive or more active; sweeter or more bitter, etc. These are words that only you can understand in relationship to the taste you have experienced. All blending, as tasting, has to be done on this very personal basis.

You may decide that the blend is going in the direction you would like or that you have over-stepped by one ingredient. It is very much as the Bible says, 'seeing through a glass darkly'. (Remember the chart at the beginning of Chapter five on taste and smell qualities, strengths, etc.) Good blending is a combination of instinct, planning for the expected and being prepared to take advantage of the unexpected. In other words, seeing things with rather more of an instinct than a certainty.

Not only do plants, in relationship to each other, affect the medicinal balance (discussed in Chapter six) but two strong flavours can, together, produce a light, delicate taste. A bitter herb in conjunction with another bitter herb can become quite sweet and palatable. This is because of the interaction of the chemical constituents, in some cases cancelling and in other cases reinforcing. If, having finally arrived at a satisfactory blend, a little embellishment is desired, then the addition of essential oils is required and my choice for this mixture might be any that we have previously discussed. Using a dropper bottle, add with tremendous caution, remembering their great strength and, likewise, medicinal and flavour potency. Upon tasting this well-stirred tea, one may decide that a symphony has been born, or that many delicate flavours have been overpowered with the use of the essential oil to the detriment of the drink.

If you have achieved a herb tea which is delighting your palate, it is now important to translate those pinches into quantifiable weights. One pinch could represent 50mg, for instance. Your guesswork may be pretty well correct but your test is the original tea and both this and any further 'matching' attempts should be drunk at the same temperature and same infusion length, as different temperatures and different infusions produce different flavours. If you have a more orderly mind than my own, you may have started with exact weights to begin with and this second stage may become almost unnecessary.

Sweetness
Finally, the thing that can alter the taste of your herb tea yet again is the introduction of added sweetness. I, personally, like to leave my cups of herb tea to brew for at least 15 minutes in order to extract the last drop of goodness. If the recipe contains any slightly bitter herbs, then their bitterness will have been brought out by this lengthy infusion, and it is then that the introduction of honey can bring about a balance of flavour. It may not necessarily make it sweet, just harmonious. As previously discussed in Chapter four, every brand, type and jar of honey has a different flavour: some are strong, some organic, some polluted, some weak, some almost tasteless, but all can alter the flavour of the herb tea.

Other additions to the herb tea would be lemon or orange. Otherwise, a basic tea can be altered according to ones mood by the addition of, say, a clove or some crumbled cinnamon.

The making of beverages from plants, roots and barks has either been a rudimentary activity, without grace or ritual, or a carefully considered and exciting adventure into the unknown. Blending combinations of plants might seem, on the surface, tedious and unnecessary but it is a very important part of getting to know the herbs as individuals and how they react alongside their companions. You are now a stage nearer to unlocking a door to unusual new drinks. Once you have made a blend which is your own, which not only you but your friends enjoy, you will have found, perhaps, both a taste-bud companion and a medicinal protector for life – surely well worth the effort.

The actual science of blending herb tea recipes will be discussed in

Chapter six. However, what you have hopefully learned so far is an instinctive approach to blending through tasting and mixing. It was this method that taught me about blending herb teas. The lessons learned in this chapter will be more appropriate to the kind of recipes and ideas aired in Chapter seven, but do bear them in mind when using the medicinal formulas in Chapter six.

Natural healers
Herbs for health, beauty and body maintenance

Matching the herbs with the symptoms

Having already discussed the growing of herbs, their care in the soil, their visual appearance, how carefully they must be picked and, if bought dried, how choosy one must be, it is now time to move on and peer more closely at their other qualities.

As everyone knows, herbs have a far-flung range of medicinal virtues and most people like to fit those characters to a symptom or illness. So often one hears, 'I've got arthritis. Which herb shall I take?' Now the answer to that question is that it won't be just one herb but many, and the second question should be, 'Why have you got arthritis' and 'Have you got any other illnesses or body disharmony?'

Some people know that faulty diet and lack of exercise are the reasons for most illnesses but hope to ignore the fact, opting for the use of herbs simply because they are natural. However, what they are in fact doing is mentally replacing herbs with drugs from their GPs. The trap of herbs and symptom matching is a trap all too easily fallen into. So, before discussing any medicinal recipes, the philosophy behind which herbs to choose should be firmly understood.

Diagnosis and formulation

The language used to describe an illness or condition tends to hold pride of place amongst most doctors and its diagnosis is truly obsessive, while the perpetual cycle of isolating a problem and trying to change or control it remains paramount in allopathic medicine. Sadly, this avenue is often explored by those practising alternative medicine, merely replacing the herb for a drug, as stated earlier. Precise, analytical diagnosis is as dangerous as framing the wrong man for a crime. Diagnosis is certainly not the province of the lay person either and should not be attempted. If you are lucky enough to have had someone who can truly wholistically diagnose, then fine. Otherwise, be very careful, play safe, and use gentle mixtures of herbs of which I shall talk more.

What any herbal formula should do is restore harmony in all areas of the body, producing an acceleration of healthy bodily functioning, enabling the body, in time, to heal itself. Alongside this, general balancing and detoxification of the body is paramount. Firstly, the main channel of elimination *must* be cleaned, which is the bowel, also the liver stimulated to excrete its toxins, the kidneys to flush their liquids, and the lymphatic system and bloodstream honed to function at top pitch, purifying and cleansing throughout. It is also possible, if one wishes, to add herbs that will aid a described symptom. Sleeplessness, for instance, can be helped, but only as part of the whole problem, in other words, treating the symptom as part of a totality. Even the herbs for sleeplessness will not be in the form of a drug 'sledgehammer', which immediately sends the patient to sleep and which only functions and gives results while the drug is being taken. No, the patient will be supported with nervine herbs but also given herbs rich in calcium, vitamin D (vitamin D is needed in order to absorb calcium, while calcium sheaths the nerve endings and rebuilds the nervous system) and many more. In fact, this treatment may take some time to re-establish a good healthy sleeping pattern but it will be a long-term repair of the problem. This is because a disease healed naturally leaves a person stronger and gives rise to a true understanding of why the illness occurred, due to the slower healing rate. This is the basis of preventative medicine.

Herbal personalities

Herbs themselves are as complex as human beings and their relationship to mankind is very interesting. As I fleetingly mentioned at the end of Chapter one, the Chinese and other herbalists now place herb characters into Yin and Yang (male and female, hot and cold, etc) and these can be used to complement or balance the person mentally and physically.

For instance, if the person is hot, aggressive and rather speedy, some calming, cooling and detoxifying herbs could be applied. These are generally tender leaves and petals (above ground) like hibiscus, chamomile, elderflower, mint, etc. Someone who appears to have poor circulation and who is weak, thin, cold, negative and repressed would be given roots and barks like dandelion, burdock, cherry bark and ginseng, which will affect the deeper organs.

This balancing method touches both mind and soul and seeks to perform positive psychology without the aid of a couch and analyst. All herbs contain both Yin and Yang, just like people, but this state in plants, as in people, is fluid and changeable to some degree. This logo picture explains the concept.

Yang

Yin

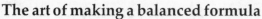

The art of making a balanced formula

There are many different reasons and causes which bring about illness: stress, worry, overwork, shock, excessive childbirth, inherited faults, to name just some. There should preferably be as many herbs to match those reasons within a formula, to produce a multiple series of effects. All herbs are potent to a greater or lesser degree and therefore a mixture dilutes the more potent ones, while still using their strength. Using single herbs may have an effect that is too direct or too strong.

Mixing herbs produces subtle changes within each one with shades not otherwise found in the single herb, the whole combination ensuring harmony and balance. Some herbs are very hot, male and dominant (Yang), like ginger, while others are watery, female and cold (Yin), such as mint. As discussed earlier, these herbs can be mixed according to the person they are to be given to in order to bring about a change. Otherwise, a balanced formula is always desirable for general use.

Some herbs are balanced within themselves, containing both Yin and Yang, for instance, devil's claw (*harpagophytum procumbens*). Its diuretic, water-eliminative properties can be seen as Yin, but to balance this there is the very Yang character (quickly shown up by its bitterness), useful for liver and gall bladder complaints. Beyond this, copious water elimination puts a strain upon the blood circulation and the Yang principles provide the necessary heart-strengthening characteristics to balance this. The bitter quality in any herb signifies stimulation and detoxification and wherever they are used there should always be sufficient Yin herbs to balance them. However, because bitter herbs are not very palatable in a tea, I have not included too many! But I have always sought balance in all the standard recipes given here.

Using herbs that complement each other means that if anything in the formula is very strong, there should always be a buffer. With spicy or pungent herbs, for instance, the irritating effects should always be balanced with a demulcent herb: cayenne pepper and marshmallow would be just that partnership. Or if heavily laxative and diuretic herbs are used, an astringent should be added to tone down the effect. For this reason, when any of the tea formulas are being made by a lay person it is important to obtain exactly the herb mentioned in exactly the correct proportion. Only a skilled herbalist would know what substitutes were possible.

Most tea formulas have a main component similarity, although they do differ slightly according to the illness one is faced with, but I shall deal with these subtle differences as we come to them. So, as a general outline of formula proportions, this is what you should have . . .

1. A large proportion of one to three herbs that possess the primary objective of the tea (it should form the major bulk of the herb tea). Although each primary herb may be very similar in its action, all are slightly different and a balance can be maintained due to this.

2. A small amount of an antispasmodic herb should be added – these are herbs that relieve nervous irritability and reduce or prevent excessive involuntary muscular contractions or spasms. In general terms, they reduce any tension within the body, working physically and emotionally on the patient.

3. A small amount of a stimulant herb should be added as this helps direct the action of the primary herbs. My teacher, Dr Christopher, called these 'thinking herbs'.

4. Finally, a small amount of carminative or demulcent herb should be added to counteract any harsh or irritating activities – for instance, the harsh diuretic action of juniper berries or horsetail should always be mellowed with the very mucilaginous marshmallow, Iceland moss or comfrey. They also generally help assimilation by softening and relaxing internal organs.

Here is a very simple tea to show the basic structure.

A tea for toothache
Parts

3 Plantain (leaf)	
3 Hops (flower)	Primaries
2 Chamomile (flower)	
1 Clove	Antispasmodic
1 Meadowsweet (leaf)	Carminative and demulcent
1 Cayenne (pepper)	Stimulant

Plus addition of chamomile essential oil (1ml) or half a drop

Apart from the structure of a formula, its action takes a specific form on many levels and all factors should be included.

Firstly — elimination and de-toxification must be considered, using:

Laxative herbs
Blood purifying herbs   All to varying degrees, according to the patient's physical state.
Diuretic herbs
Diaphoretic herbs

Secondly — support and maintenance of the body should accompany the above process, using such herbs as analgesics to reduce pain, etc.

Thirdly — building and toning is vital, and nerve and liver tonics are needed: see *Sleep and nerve tonic* and *Liver and gall bladder tea*.

Actual application of all these factors requires yet more thought and direction, according to the particular patient. There are basically eight therapeutic approaches, which are:

Stimulation
Blood purification
Tonification
Purging
Tranquillisation
Diuresis
Emesis
Sweating

By merely knowing of the presence of these many factors when making a herbal formula, a cautionary lesson may have been gleaned: a little knowledge is dangerous.

Cautionary notes on herb uses
Take all herb teas for six days, resting on the seventh with fruit juices.

Sassafras (whole herb)	Do not use during pregnancy: cease use after three to four weeks.
Horsetail (whole herb)	Delete from recipe after four weeks, replacing with dandelion. Always rest the tea on the seventh day.
Poke root	Use for six days only and then not for another three to six months; a very strong herb.
Ginseng (root) Liquorice (root)	Both stimulate heart action: do not use in cases of high blood pressure
Hawthorn berries	Delete in cases of low blood pressure.
Lime tree flower	Care should be taken over freshness of supplies. Old, slightly fermented leaves can cause hallucinations.
Chamomile (flower)	If this is taken too strongly or infused for too long, it will cause nausea. This is important for children's doses. This is why this herb is best in a combination, rather than drunk singly.

Note: Nausea is the body's safety mechanism. If it is ever experienced during the drinking of any herbal tea, either drink less or dilute the quantity. This is often the body's way of telling that the dose is not required. It may even mean that the formula should be changed altogether.

Extra cayenne for both high and low blood pressure is very beneficial.

Prevention instead of cure

Ancient healing at its highest and most advanced form made no attempt to cure disease at all. The road it took was to sustain the individual during his or her period of disability, using mild foods (fasts, herbs and positive mental attitudes, often in the form of spiritual disciplines). Not a thought was given to offering a remedy that might interfere with the natural processes and manifestation of illness. General balancing herbs were prescribed to promote the natural functions of the body and to strengthen from within.

Causes of diseases

Diseases have many causes. These can stem from physiological factors, affecting the tissues and the blood – in other words our physical make up – which need diagnosis on a physical plane. Or they can stem from what we can call biological factors, meaning the food we eat, its cultivation and its processing. They can also stem from ecological factors – our environment and the way it affects us, as well as nature and her seasons. Finally, they can stem from psychological factors – possibly the largest category of all in the causation of disease – which affect all the spiritual, emotional and mental aspects of our well-being.

For these reasons, the drinking of herbal teas goes only some way towards relieving or treating an illness. It is most important, therefore, to work with a practitioner for the overall treatment of a problem. In this chapter we are really only dealing with physiological and biological factors, although obviously drinking herbs instead of coffee or tea does go some way towards altering the emotions and the psyche.

The correct diet

As we are discussing general good health and those herbal teas used to sustain it, we must briefly discuss the correct diet to go with it as 'all the herb tea in China' will not produce a healthy body if toxins, in the form of the wrong food, are being absorbed in the first place.

This diet outline is a generalisation and not tailored to special needs; seek advice from your practitioner for this.

Food to cut out	*Their substitutes*
White bread	Wholemeal brown bread (local wheat, organic, stone-ground), unleavan bread or some cereal breads.
White flours	Potato flour, rice flour, soya flour, arrowroot, etc.

Food to cut out	*Their substitutes*
Milk, cheese, eggs	Soya milk, tofu, occasionally egg or egg yolk in balance.
Red meats	Chicken, lamb, turkey, fish, or no meat at all, but if no meats are eaten then adequate B vitamins, especially B_{12}, should be taken, i.e., comfrey tea. (All meats should be free-range, organically fed.)
Tea and coffee, alcohol	Herb tea, occasional sip of purest of all alcohol and therefore less toxic i.e. vodka.

Additions to the diet

Long and low-cook or gently heat everything in order to preserve the foods' life force.

Sprouted beans and seed (1 to ½ cupful a day).

Steam cook vegetables, leaving skins on, or eat raw.

Drink vegetable juices and fruit juices.

Generally combine herbs and spices in your daily food.

Vitamins and minerals

These words are on the lips and in the minds of many people today and sadly most feel that they need to indulge in expensive vitamins and minerals from a pill jar. These are synthetic reproductions of the natural thing and, I feel, used only as a last resort or in times of chronic or acute illness or for those who will not use the 'real thing'.

Synthetic vitamins and minerals are, in the main, rapidly eliminated through the urine and wasted, or, worse still, remain lodged and harmful in the liver or kidneys. This is easy to understand when the construction of a man-made vitamin or mineral pill is examined. It may contain excipients, binders, fillers, lubricants, disintegrants, slow release and colouring agents and agents for preserving the capsule shell. These are all quite legally exempt from being listed on the ingredients label, no matter what percentage they take up of the finished product. Of course, some of the actual vitamin and mineral content is organic, but very often the bulk is in-organic, making the entire pill completely useless and, worse, harmful.

A person's initial deficiency of vitamins and minerals is due to an imbalance and poor assimilation, or too rapid an elimination in the first place, possibly due to a long-term lack of nutrients prior to this stage. The word 'tonic' probably conjures up your grandmother and her 'quack medicine', but its application today, as ever, is highly important as it will improve the assimilation of vital nutrients by the organs, while nutritive herbs provide adequate amounts of balanced minerals and vitamins in a very assimilable form.

As for every basic recipe, I would like you to enter into my own thinking process when deciding what should go into a formula. If you can just imagine a formula as a game of hockey, say, where everybody has their particular roles to play in order to shoot a goal – right back, right inner and centre forward – this is so with the herbs themselves. One thing that also must be understood about herbs is that they have multiple functions. For instance, in the following *Vitamin, mineral and nutritive herbal tea* we are also putting in herbs which have very important roles to play beyond being excellent vitamin, mineral and nutritive agents. Comfrey, for instance, is a fine healing agent and able to form new growth cells. The body has the ability to take what it most needs and remains supreme over our own minds on these decisions. Remember, too, that vitamins and minerals can never be 'singled out' for importance as every one of them is reliant on the next for proper absorption and assimilation – hence the beauty of the multiple herbal drink.

Finally, just one caution. Every plant is reliant on the climate and soil from which it grows for its vitamin and mineral content and general plant chemistry. However, in all the years of buying herbs and using them for hundreds of patients (and bought by hundreds of customers) I have always found them to be entirely adequate, although, obviously, some are far superior to others, the less superior demanding a slightly prolonged treatment. The Chinese are the most choosy about quality, always conscious of freshness and the life force within the plant. If you are growing your own herbs on your own plot of land, then a soil test will reveal all the qualities or deficiencies, which you can then put right – although you cannot change the weather! Whether poor or rich in soil nutrients, plants of your own, lovingly culled with your own hands (or those of a loved one) are going to give you the greatest benefit and be most complementary to your body's needs.

It is frequently argued by scientists that plants' values cannot be quantified as their chemistry differs from soil to soil, weather to weather, country to country and differing times of harvest. This is absolutely so. However, as I explained earlier, the body is quite adept at taking what it needs and shedding what it does not require. The body is also structured to give out signals when something is required or if it has had enough and a balance has been reached. If we learn to read body signals or go to someone who can read them for us, a much more personal and superior approach to bodily needs than 'dosage analysis' for the masses is reached. Quantification of a known substance is only important in an allopathic approach to medicine where isolation of particular components has taken place, instabilities have arisen and often dangerous levels of potency have been reached, a state which we will obviously avoid. Quantification is also highly irrelevant as deficiencies in each person may vary dramatically and cannot be measured so specifically.

Vitamin, mineral and nutritive herbal tea
Parts

1 Kelp (or some other seaweed)	General nutritive, high in iodine and very high in calcium. Kelp, like any seaweed, contains chlorophyll and is important for oxygenation of the body.
1 Yellow dock (root)	High in iron, general nutritive.
2 Dandelion (root)	General nutritive and tonic; very high in easily assimilable minerals.
½ Parsley (root)	Vitamins A, B, iron and copper; general nutritive. Also three times as much vitamin C as citrus fruits.
3 Alfalfa (leaf)	Rather than buying dried, these are best sprouted, i.e. used fresh. This contains most known vitamins and minerals: vitamins A, D, E, K, C, B_1, B_2, B_6, B_{12}, folic acid, niacin, pantothenic acid, inositol, biotin.
1 Rosehip	Very high in vitamin C.
1 Nettle (leaf)	High in iron, also contains silicon, potassium, lime, sodium, chlorine and large amounts of protein.
1 Watercress (leaf)	Use this freshly chopped. Very rich in most known minerals, especially calcium (250mg to 25g), also iron and vitamin D.
1 Burdock (root)	General nutritive and tonic: high in iron.
2 Comfrey (leaf)	A general nutritive, high in vitamin B_{12}, especially the Bocking 14 variety from Lawrence Hills. (The allantoin of comfrey, its cell-proliferant qualities, is destroyed in boiling water, but not its vitamin and nutritive qualities.)

This tea is made up in specific proportions but I would suggest adding more rosehip if you particularly enjoy the flavour. To this tea one may add honey if you wish – remember my discourse on the pros and cons of honey in Chapter four and remember that a dark-coloured honey is high in minerals. Honey is most abundant in its source of natural chromium.

There is a particular drain on vitamins and minerals within the body in times of stress and this tea should be drunk more often during such a time.

For the individual benefits of vitamins and minerals and their importance and function in the body, read: *Minerals* by Miriam Polunin, and *Vitamins* by Carol Hunter (both published by Thorsons Ltd).

Daily health

The *Daily health tea* use herbs which support and balance the system as a daily routine. It differs from the *Vitamin, mineral and nutritive tea* in that it has blood purifying elements in it, mild and safe antibiotics, antiseptics, gentle de-toxifying herbs, and gentle stimulants. Both teas gently supplement imbalances of energy, toning deficiencies and restoring harmony in both mind and body, i.e. creating the natural interflow of Yin and Yang. You will see that roots, leaves, flowers and fruit have been used.

Daily health tea
Parts

2 Elderflower	This plant affects the blood circulation, lungs, bowels and skin. It is very cooling to the blood system, and very important for the prevention of coughs, colds and pulmonary infections.
1 Sarsaparilla (root)	This plant affects the blood, skin, circulation and intestines. A powerful tonic and blood purifier, it has anti-putrefaction properties, and contains iron, potassium, chloride, calcium and magnesium. Promotes perspiration and the flow of urine. Contains the hormones testosterone and progesterone.
2 Hibiscus (flower) (approximately) – adjust to taste)	Introduced into this formula for its acid flavouring, it also contains malic acid and vitamin C.
½ Rosemary (leaf and flower)	This affects the whole system, eliminating and stimulating. High in easily assimilable calcium, it also promotes cell growth and repair. It has the ability to dilate blood vessels and should always, therefore, be taken in balance.
1 Yellow dock (root)	As a general alterative, i.e. a blood purifier and herb that will draw out toxins, it produces a tonic effect within the system.
1 Nettle (leaf)	This affects the lungs and kidneys, bladder and blood. It aids the assimilation of minerals. It is very helpful for asthma, anaemia and bleeding.
2 Marshmallow (leaf or root)	This affects the intestines, kidneys and bladder but generally the whole body. High nutritive, like rosemary, it produces cell growth and repair and is the best source of easily digested vegetable mucilage, which lubricates joints and regulates the heat of the body. High in lime and calcium; roots high in oxygen and pectin.

83

2 Raspberry (leaf)	This plant affects the stomach, liver, blood, genito-urinary tract and muscles, and soothes and tones the tissue of stomach and bowels. High in iron, it's generally a very 'female herb'.
½ Thyme (leaf)	Very healing and antiseptic, a famous component to all throat gargles and bronchial problems. Has a soothing action on nerves and eliminates odours – a natural deodorant. Highly antiseptic.
½ Sage (leaf)	Like thyme, sage is antispasmodic, but its main function is in slowing the secretions of fluids (an astringent), therefore it is useful for excessive perspiration, diarrhoea, early stages of colds and 'flu, sinus congestion, etc. It's also a wonderful gargle, like thyme.
1 Wild cherry bark	This plant affects the upper respiratory system, liver and stomach. It is very helpful for coughs and sore throats, for improving digestion and influencing the liver and secretion of bile.
½ Cayenne (pepper)	Cayenne is the most superior tonic and daily herb as well as being an indispensable crisis herb. It affects the whole body helping the heart, circulation, preventing heart attacks, strokes, colds, 'flu, lethargy, headaches, indigestion, depression and arthritis, and more.
2 Agrimony (leaf)	This plant affects the liver, blood and skin. One of the finest liver cleansers, it has the power to cure jaundice.

Use 25g per 600ml boiling water. Infuse for 15 minutes or more. I suggest adding your own honey or Spanish rosemary.

As you will see with this tea, most organs of the body have been gently stimulated to excrete toxins, while flushing the liver and kidneys, and cleansing the lymphatic system, bloodstream and skin. The whole system has been toned, healed and cells repaired just like any good maintenance programme.

Prevention of illness using herbs does include special categories beyond servicing the body in a normal daily fashion. Sometimes the body is quite well but naturally healthy extra pressures are placed on it – for instance, becoming pregnant. So, still under the banner of *Prevention instead of cure*, but also as a separate heading for early reference, comes pregnancy and post-natal care of the mother, which I then follow up with herbal teas for the growing baby, toddler and young child.

Note: It is wise to give all herb teas a rest on the seventh day of the week in order to rest the body and allow a flow of toxins. Drink fruit juices.

Pregnancy and motherhood

The special needs of pregnancy are generally known, that of iron, folic acid and calcium; deficiencies in these areas cause loss of oxygen and possible brain damage to the growing foetus and anaemia to the mother, preventing bone cell and tissue formation. Beyond iron and calcium, general nutritive plants are important for the general 'drain' on the body, peak health being most important for both baby and mother. If this tea can be taken just before conception then so much the better. If not, it should be drunk as soon as the pregnancy is suspected or confirmed.

The first three months in the growth of the foetus are the most important, laying down the blue-print upon which the rest of the pregnancy grows. If this blue-print is badly deficient then natural abortion often occurs at this time, which is a fortunate thing, but this loss can sometimes be unnecessary due to inadequate rest, diet and feeding of the very young foetus. So let us prevent this possibility.

Note: Foods like fenugreek, kelp, rice bran, tinned and fresh fish, Brewers' yeast, whole grains and beetroot and carrot juice would be helpful allies to this tea as all B vitamins are vital, especially folic acid, plus plenty of calcium, vitamins A and D, and zinc.

Pre-natal tisane – 'Motherhood tea'

Parts

1 Blessed thistle (leaf)	Blood purifier and tonic. General female herb.
2 Raspberry (leaf)	Major active principle is fragrine, which has a special influence in the uterus and its muscles; helps morning sickness. Vital for health of mother and embryo. Contains iron and nutrients needed from conception to birth. Helps to prevent miscarriage.
1 Horsetail (foliage)	High silica and calcium, provokes emptying of the bladder, so low quantity.
3 Comfrey (leaf or root)	Vitamin B content, and folic acid important for nervous system, morning sickness. Cell-proliferant qualities of allantoin vital for forming the baby. High calcium.
1 Nettle (leaf)	Nettles are vital for the body to assimilate the calcium plants and other minerals. High iron, about 45 per cent of plant.
1 Marshmallow (leaf or root)	High in easily assimilated calcium. Nutritive and tonic. Natural calcium is vital as inorganic calcium, e.g. pills are non-assimilable in general and contain no nourishment, clogging the system up.

85

1 Sarsaparilla (root)	Contains hormones; high in iron and calcium.
2 Yellow dock (root)	One of the best blood builders in nature due to its 4 per cent iron compounds. Both sarsaparilla and dock are excellent blood purifiers.
1 Allspice or ginger (root)	Both calm the stomach, keeping morning sickness to a minimum, both helpful for the bowels. Strengthening to the spleen.
1 Cinnamon (shredded)	Helpful for morning sickness.
1 Liquorice (shredded)	A mild, safe and effective laxative, helpful for constipation problems sometimes experienced in pregnancy. It also contains the female hormone, oestrogen. Adds a lovely flavour to whole tea and helps with any nausea. Do not use if hypertensive.

Note: Nausea or vomiting during pregnancy is fairly common, often starting after the sixth week and lasting for four to six weeks. If, however, it is more pronounced or goes on during most of the pregnancy, then other deficiencies should be looked at, i.e. excess mucus, a weak stomach/spleen or gastric/bile imbalances: use relevant teas in this chapter for these symptoms. This kind of sickness will reflect itself in your particular deficiency, i.e. a mucus sickness or bitter fluid sickness, containing bile.

Make this tea below boiling point, i.e. boil water and when just below boiling point pour on to herbs (by measuring once and tasting heat you will be able to gauge this fairly accurately thereafter). Boiling water kills the allantoin in the comfrey which is vital here for the growing baby. For persistent vomiting of pregnant women, add one part Chinese ginseng to this formula, but not if hypertensive (also leave out the liquorice).

You will notice that a lot of these herbs occur in the *Vitamin, mineral and nutritive herbal tea* and *Daily health tea*, so amongst their specific pregnancy attributes, they have these benefits, too.

Having given birth and if you are, hopefully, contemplating breast-feeding, it is important to see that there is sufficient milk of superior quality for the baby.

Post-natal tea
Parts

1 Horsetail (foliage)	High calcium (as before).
1 Borage (leaf)	Calcium source.
1 Dandelion (root)	Liver and blood purifier; high calcium and iron.
1 Nettle (leaf)	As before.
1 Comfrey (root or leaf)	As before.
1 Vervain (foliage)	A fine milk enricher, calming and soothing.
1 Fennel (seed or leaf)	A known galactagogue (milk enricher), also helpful for wind in the baby.

1 Dill (seed)	A known galactagogue and helpful for wind in the baby (raw ingredient of gripe water).
3 Blessed thistle (leaf)	As before.
3 Raspberry (leaf)	As before.
3 Marshmallow (leaf or root)	As before.
3 Kelp	High in calcium.
2 Sassafras (root)	Tonic after childbirth, and general blood purifier.

Note: Do not use during pregnancy and remove from tea formula after three weeks.

You will see that a lot of the pregnancy herbs have been repeated due to their nutritive, iron and calcium content but the quantity of blessed thistle, red raspberry and marshmallow has been increased due to its specific galactagogue qualities. Introduced also are herbs which will help with wind and cholic. Due to this tea, my own baby practically never suffered from these problems and if I was ever slightly run down through not resting enough I made myself a stronger version of this tea for an almost instant milk shower and general revival of health!

Tea for increased milk
Blessed thistle
Red raspberry leaves } Equal parts
Marshmallow root

Do not infuse in boiling water, but soak the herbs, 25g to 600ml, in cold water for several hours.

I suggest both teas are combined with apple juice (fresh or concentrate) for flavour and a useful alkaline addition to the body. Remember that citrus fruits reduce milk flow and are best introduced in weaning along with sage tea, made as a steeped cold infusion.

Now to the baby, and eventual toddler itself. Soon it will drink from a bottle or feeder as well as from the mother, and I have a lovely recipe for settling, soothing and nourishing even the youngest of babies, tried and tested on my own and hundreds of others. The first tea is for babies under six months, as they should only receive very mild herbs, while the second is for those babies over six months, where stronger herbs can be gently introduced.

Babies' tea (under six months)
Equal parts

Lemon balm	Calming, soothing, ideal for wind and indigestion.
Catnip (leaf)	Calming, soothing.

Babies' tea (over six months)
Parts

½ Chamomile (flower)	Very soothing to the nervous system. Ideal for colds, teething, depressed appetite. (Excessive dose produces nausea so use small amount in formula).
2 Catnip (leaf)	Cholic soother and general aromatic nervine (tonic and healer for the nerves). Helpful for teething problems, etc.
½ Marshmallow (leaf)	Apart from its attributes previously mentioned, it is helpful for flatulent cholic.
2 Parsley (seed)	Helpful for stomach and bowel pains, aches, cramp, etc. Nutritive herb.
2 Caraway (seed)	Similar to above.
1 Dill (seed)	Natural 'gripe water'.

Add honey to sweeten, though this is probably unnecessary, also kelp if taste is acceptable. Use pinch of tea for 275-300ml water, administered over an entire day.

As the baby becomes a young toddler, grows older and breast-feeding draws to an end, then the source of natural antibiotics, calcium, iron and general nourishment gained from the mother's milk also ceases. In general, food will be a replacement for all this, but a good standard tea that your toddler or child has learnt to drink from an early age is the best idea. It will ensure healthy teeth development with as few teething problems as possible, strong bone formation and a generally healthy approach to life and its illnesses, which will surround the child, but hopefully, not touch him or her. Beyond this, problems of cholic and wind should subside with the development of the internal organs.

Dosage for children

The dose for a child between one and three years old should be well below an adult's, i.e. use roughly one teaspoon to half a pint of water.

As herb teas are food, the sensible approach is that the teas should be all relevant to food intake, and spread across the day. So, with babies over one year old I would suggest that either the *Daily health tea* or *Vitamin, mineral and nutritive herbal tea* were ideal, both containing antiseptics, mild antibiotics, nutritives, calcium, iron, and many other vitamins. My personal choice would be to alternate these two teas, leaving one day a week where the child had just fruit juices, preferably apple juice. All this interspaced with plenty of purified water.

To make these teas more acceptable or exciting, one could add liquorice, often used to disguise strong or bitter flavours and naturally very sweet (also a very mild and age-old laxative), or spearmint or carob powder, which is a powder made from a tree pod, often used as a chocolate substitute and found in wholefood and healthfood shops; carob is also highly nutritive.

Do not forget the honey. Remember also, however, that even though babies, toddlers and children have a naturally sweet tooth it is often far less sweet than we, as adults, assume it is and, of course, they need far less than an adult. However, honey will never over-burden the pancreas, unlike all other sugars, as it naturally causes nausea and a lack of appetite should it ever get to this level. But never force sweetened food or drink.

Building and cleansing

We are now leaving behind daily, preventative medicine-type teas and moving on to the second phase in self-bodycare, which is of cleansing and re-conditioning all the main systems and organs. As my teacher, Dr Christopher says, one can be constipated throughout the body not just in the bowel area! The bloodstream, with its tiny veins and connecting arteries, easily becomes obstructed or sluggish, causing problems varying from feeling cold to fibrous cysts and heart attacks. We are familiar enough with taking laxatives when we're constipated but not so conscious of doing the same for all the other eliminative channels and organs; the lymphatic system, blood system, lungs, liver, kidneys, skin and spleen. Once these *cleansing teas* have performed their function it is wise to return once again to the *preventative teas* for daily use. Because these are particularly cleansing to the various systems, it is very important to rest from these one day a week and so drink these teas six days to release toxins on the seventh.

Many people may ask, 'How do you know when my cleansing programme has finished?' The answer is, really, when you feel better. To judge this, keep a diary and note any improvement – it's so easy to get better and hardly notice wellbeing. Some people may feel flushed out in a matter of a week, while others may take six months, but it is always important to drink fruit juices and water alongside the cleansing teas in order to assist in the body-washing process and so that the body doesn't 'overwork' too quickly.

The healing crisis
There is a law of cure which frequently follows a pattern called the healing crisis. This means feeling worse before you feel better. It occurs when the body acts to repel the cause of the disease, whatever its nature.

A healing crisis can take many forms. It can appear when the illness is growing, but is more likely to occur quite suddenly in the last stage of disease. The crisis is the last chance for the body to eliminate all toxins. It can affect the body physically, mentally and emotionally. When the healing crisis occurs all stimulation should stop. All eating should cease and any laxative or emetic herbs should be avoided – they merely weaken the body's own natural healing mechanism.

Anything from vomiting and diarrhoea to nosebleeds, headaches and perspiration may be experienced. Warning signals are heat, pain, swelling and headache. If at this acute stage the healing crisis is allowed to develop, the body will not need to go through a more strenuous healing crisis, brought on by chronic illness, at a later stage. Although uncomfortable at the time, the healing crisis signals that recovery is close at hand.

The bowel

As we have talked so often about constipation, it is time, I think, we explored the subject more fully. The cause of most intestinal and bowel complaints is bad eating habits, like the cause of most problems. Highly processed and refined foods, and milk, cheese and wheat produce create a great deal of mucus in the intestine which sticks to the walls of these tubes, gluing itself like wallpaper paste. Just like wallpaper in old houses, there are many layers, the result in the lower bowel being a very much reduced thickness of tubing for which the faecal matter can pass through. This produces several problems, the most immediate being constipation, but a stage worse is when the faecal matter automatically remains watery, giving the appearance of not being constipated whereas the situation is that the clogged tracts block any absorption of the ingested foods. Worse still, this thick, hardened, layered mucus ring becomes so heavy that the bowel weakens, loses its elasticity and balloons out – terms like diviticulitis and prolapse will be familiar to some who have reached this stage. Beyond all this, poisons have not been properly eliminated. Even with very infrequent constipation problems, toxins flood back into the system (particularly dangerous during pregnancy and this can penetrate through the walls of the womb).

A cleansed bowel means better food assimilation, increased vitality and nutrition levels and often a decreased desire to eat as much food. In a chronic bowel condition, often only 10 per cent of food intake can be utilised.

With this tea, the aim is *not* to give large amounts of laxatives but to re-build the bowel structure and regain peristaltic muscle movement so that the bowel can work properly of its own accord. Almost everybody needs a bowel cleanse, and this is the first place to start, whatever the illness or complaint – being the major eliminative channel.

Beyond this mild tea, Dr Christopher has a wonderful 'lower bowel formula', most of which is rather bitter and, therefore, powdered and

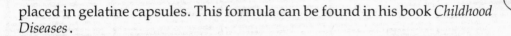

placed in gelatine capsules. This formula can be found in his book *Childhood Diseases*.

Bowel building tea
Parts

3 Ginger (root)	Wonderful stimulant to the whole system, and helps 'activate' the other herbs. Excellent for relieving and correcting cramps, pains and flatulence.
1 Dill (seed)	Tasty and excellent for flatulence.
1 Fennel (seed or foliage)	Helpful for flatulence, indigestion, cramps, spasms, pinworms and general liver malfunctions.
2 Sage (leaf)	A laxative, very helpful for flatulence.
1 Cayenne (pepper)	Slightly laxative, it stimulates the organs (like ginger) it passes through, cleansing and re-building all. Helpful in the removal of mucus.
2 Liquorice (shredded)	A mild laxative, it is also a de-toxifier.
1 Red raspberry (leaf)	This herb is an astringent, acting on the contraction of internal tissues and membranes – this is due to its citrate of iron content and blood-making regulating properties.
1 Comfrey (root)	As a cell-proliferant this will re-build the walls of the bowel and intestine, its mucilaginous qualities protecting the bowel from harsh effects of food fibre during the rebuilding process.
1 Marigold (flower)	An emollient which relieves pain from cell deterioration in chronic bowel conditions. Otherwise, generally healing and restoring all it comes in contact with. Comfrey and marigold work well together. Helpful for piles, fissures, etc.
1 Blackthorn flowers (*prunus spinosa*)	Safe and gentle purgative.

An excellent addition to this tea for flavour is carob (*ceratonia siliqua*). Combined with honey its taste is very similar to chocolate and can easily be passed off as a chocolate drink – lovely in winter!

The bloodstream

Of course, the most difficult thing to establish very often is whether one's liver needs a jolly good flush or whether the kidneys are acting sluggishly. However, every culture in every kind of medicine readily accepts that diagnosis is the most difficult task of all and I am certainly not preparing to indulge you in a crash course now. You will need some help on this matter.

So let us deal with what is most obvious. For instance, people worry a great deal if their skin is in a bad condition, e.g. acne, spots, blotches, dryness. It is readily visible to themselves and everybody else, perhaps parallel to constipation. However, most people generally approach the problem from the outside instead of from within. A very simple suggestion here would be to cleanse the bloodstream.

The important functions of the blood are supplying nutrients to body tissues, removing the waste products of the body's metabolism, transporting hormones and participating in the immunization process. It is very closely linked to the lymphatic system (see later) which includes the lymph nodes, the spleen and lymphatic tissue in the bone marrow.

When cleaning the bowel it is also essential to clean the bloodstream. The two should always be part of the same process.

Blood purifying tea

Parts

3 Burdock (chopped root)	Major blood purifier, natural antibiotic.
1 Red clover (flower and leaf)	Generally alterative, it is also a mild stimulant, slightly sedative, and able to remove obstructions and act as a detergent; potent healing properties.
1 Dandelion (chopped root)	As before.
1 Sassafras (chopped root)	Do not use during pregnancy, cease use after three weeks and replace with extra red clover.
1 Sarsaparilla (chopped root)	Excellent skin and circulation tonic and blood purifier; contains iron and promotes sweating and the flow of urine.
1 Nettle (leaf)	High in iron, contains silicon, potassium, lime, sodium chlorine and large amounts of protein.
2 Yellow dock (chopped root)	High in iron and general nutritive and alterative; it draws out toxins and provides a tonic effect.
½ Liquorice (shredded root)	Excellent blood de-toxifier.
1 Echinacea (shredded root)	Finest antibiotic available.
½ Yarrow (in small quantity due to its bitterness – flower and leaf)	A general diaphoretic, i.e. produces sweat which is a tonic and non-exhaustive.

Note: For people with specific problems, like acne, extra yarrow should be included as it stabilises the action of the sebaceous gland.

You are by now familiar with most of these herbs but the proportions in this combination of herbs is the important factor: large proportions of some herbs and minor of others (as explained in Chapter five).

A good honey to go with this herbal tea would be red clover honey, for obvious reasons.

While we are on the subject of blood, a great many people suffer from poor circulation – cold hands and feet in particular – so here is a very *hot* tea.

Blood circulation tea
Parts
1½ Rosemary (leaf)
½ Lavender (flower)
½ Parsley (leaf)
2 Ginger (dried flakes or
fresh root)
1 Cayenne (place powder
in muslin bag)
1 Sassafras   Do not using during pregnancy – cease use after
(chopped root)   three weeks and replace with red clover or
                              ginseng.

All these ingredients have been previously discussed. This tea would be lovely made with buckwheat honey, which is tasty and helpful for strengthening the arteries.

The upper respiratory system

We are now going to move further up the body to what we might broadly call the upper respiratory system. This can cover the lungs and throat and ailments connected with these: sore throats, asthma, bronchitis, catarrh, etc., but most of all the aim is to cleanse and return all to a better function. A lot of this tea's job is to remove excess mucus, the long-term or even short-term build-up of which causes asthma, blocked sinuses, colds, coughs and tonsil inflammation. (It's initial build-up being due to a congested bowel).

In a normal functioning body, mucus is produced as a protective barrier on the surfaces of membranes, but with irritation it is over-produced – a familiar example to most people is when we have a cold, excessive mucus is produced. Mucus also attracts and harbours germs due to its sticky make-up and it is easy to see why throat and ear infections often follow a mucus overflow! Therefore, in the tea we will not only have herbs to calm the mucus membranes and to cut phlegm but also to increase the flow of saliva and mucus – decongestants – but also those herbs that will act as antibiotics and antiseptics.

Food is greatly to blame for most problems and, certainly, specific foods cause the over production of mucus, like gluten products, i.e. wheat, barley, oats, cheese, milk, to mention the most obvious ones.

Upper respiratory tisane

Parts

3 Coltsfoot (flower and leaf)	Very helpful to the lungs in general, aiding bad coughs, asthma and bronchitis.
2 Iceland moss	Excellent for chronic pulmonary problems: tuberculosis, chronic catarrh. Tonic virtues due to its cetarin content.
2 Horehound (foliage)	Effective for all pulmonary complaints as an expectorant, tonic and diaphoretic; helps relieve all congestions in that area.
2 Wild cherry (bark)	Remedy for all catarrhal affections, being a general tonic, soothing yet slightly astringent to the mucus membranes.
2 Sage (leaf)	A cure for affections of the mouth, inflamed sore throat, relaxed throat and tonsils. Helpful for sinus congestions.
1 Violets (flower)	Dissolves mucus; expectorant.
3 Mullein (leaf)	Anti-asthmatic, anti-catarrhal, this plant has a special attraction for respiratory organs and general pulmonary disorders. Being narcotic yet unharmful, it is an excellent pain killer, calming and soothing, ideal for asthmatics. Most important herb for influencing the glandular system, helping to absorb morbid accumulations.
1 Echinacea (root)	Acts as the finest antibiotic to remedy infection. (Should be left out of tea if used long term).
1 Vervain (leaf)	Good for feverish pleurisy as it induces sweating and relaxes. It is also helpful for colds, 'flu and coughs, greatly helping to expel mucus.
1 Marshmallow (root and leaf)	Soothing and healing to the mucus membrane, ideal for coughs and general pulmonary complaints.
1 Chickweed (leaf)	Excellent remedy for pulmonary complaints for any inflammation of the mucus membrane – asthma, bronchitis.
1 Comfrey (root and leaf)	Helpful in excessive expectoration of asthma, also coughs, inflamed lung conditions, bronchitis, pneumonia. It soothes and heals all inflamed tissue.

1 Sarsaparilla (root)	Breaks up mucus and phlegm.
1 Liquorice (rhizome)	Soothing and softening to the mucus membrane, especially if inflamed, good for catarrhal infection, especially of respiratory tract. It increases flow of saliva and mucus, acting as a decongestant. Helpful for sore throats.
1 Raspberry leaves	Very helpful for sore throats by its astringent yet mucilaginous, relaxant qualities.
2 Aniseed ⎫ 1 Ginger ⎭	Both act as an anti-mucus congestant, while warming and stimulating.

Note: With a practitioner's guidance, some lobelia (600ml-1.2l) could be added to this tea.

As you will realise, this is a fairly broad-spectrum tea but capable of helping so many problems in that area, if not all. For a really good dose, use 25g to 600ml of water, drinking three cups a day, or make it weaker and have five cups a day. Sweeten with Mexican organic honey.

The lymphatic system

Closely allied with the mucus membrane is the lymphatic system (which is also closely linked with the bloodstream). This system consists of a fine, thin-walled network of vessels which carry lymph (a fine, clear fluid) and these vessels are interrupted by lymph nodes which filter off bacteria and other foreign particles, giving back antibodies, apart from other things a local defence mechanism. These nodes become inflamed either before an infection is noticed or just after it has subsided, but their job is to protect and fight all germs within the system. However, I have known patients with permanently inflamed nodes/glands – sometimes for years.

One of the most important things to remember about the lymphatic system is that it does not have a heart, like the blood system does, to pump it all round. The lymphatic system relies on muscular exercise of the body to move it round – osmotic pressure – and so if the lymphatics become obstructed due to sluggishness, then obstructions cause proteins not to be drained from the tissues and fluid collects (oedema, or water retention). The lymph nodes also act as a barrier to prevent bacterial infection from spreading into the bloodstream. So you can see how important this system is in combatting generalised infections and diseases like glandular fever.

There are quite a few herbs which have a particular 'leaning' towards the lymphatic system and the following tea would be most helpful for aiding the system when signs of infection or indeed swollen glands or nodes are present. These nodal swellings are easy to locate, being at the sides and back of the neck, in the armpits and groins, at the root of the lungs and in the vicinity of the large veins of the abdomen and pelvis.

Maintenance of lymph glands requires higher levels of vitamins A and C and mineral zinc, with *non-use* of antibiotics which disarm mechanisms.

Lymphatic infection tea
Parts

1 Violet (flower)	Very mucilaginous and dissolvent, excellent for swollen glands.
3 Mullein (leaf)	This herb promotes the absorption of fluids which have escaped from their vessels through rupturing. It also absorbs morbid accumulations.
2 Devil's claw (root, cut)	An ancient herb used by many cultures; its action on the lymphatic system is very deobstruent and draining, partly due to its diuretic properties. It is a very balanced herb and it can be drunk on its own.
1 Echinacea (root)	Very strong antibiotic (should be left out of tea if used long term).
1 Poke (root)	This is one of the most powerful alteratives and very beneficial to any enlarged lymphatic glands (especially thyroid and spleen), which are very hard, swollen or enlarged. Also very helpful to mastitis and cancer. (Do not use for more than six months.)
1 Plantain (leaf)	This plant generally 'heals' the lymphatic system, absorbing poisons and reducing swellings. It is a 'cooling' alterative.
2 Burdock (root)	A strong antibiotic in its own right, it aids the job of the lymphatic system. It is alterative and diuretic.
1 Parsley (leaf)	Excellent for removing watery poisons, excess mucoid matter and reducing swollen or enlarged glands.

Note: Strain this tea very carefully before pouring to drink as the hairs on the mullein leaf can cause great itching in the throat, being irritative (although I have never experienced this).

The only bitter herb in this tea is devil's claw and, although not a *very* bitter herb, it is best disguised by something like Jaffa orange oil in liberal quantities or a fruit juice concentrate, but even without the masking, the results make the tea well worth the taste.

The glandular system
The glandular system is closely allied to the lymphatic system. For this reason keeping the lymphatic system working well is vital to maintaining

an actively balanced glandular system. It is the collected lymph nodes or glands that inflame when disease or an imbalance occurs. Besides this type of gland there are larger and more important glands like the sweat glands and the digestive glands. The pituitary gland, adrenal gland and thyroid gland are concerned primarily with metabolic rate or energy levels. Such things as our correct use of fats and sugar dictate their well-being which in turn affects our mental attitudes of depression or balanced happiness, our feeling of warmth or cold and the rate of healing and replacement of tissue.

Glandular regulating tea

Parts

1 Sarsaparilla (root)	Rich in natural hormones.
1 Liquorice (root)	Acts as a demulcent.
1 Ginseng (combination of Siberian, American and Korean)	Develops function of hormones and hormone balance.
1 Kelp	Highly nutritive, feeding and regulating the thyroid; contains iodine, calcium and manganese.
1 Ginger (root)	Stimulant.
3 Mullein (leaf)	Relieves any congestion.
1 Parsley (leaf)	Controls metabolism and thyroid activity.
1 Iceland moss	As above.
2 Comfrey (root)	High in B vitamins, vital for servicing of adrenals, pituitary glands and pancreas.

Organ building

Having dealt with systems, I would now like to deal with the flushing, unblocking and re-building (toning) of various major organs, whose jobs are to act as filters, regulators and organisers of the whole body. To know that these organs need your attentions, advice from a herbal practitioner is advisable. However, it would be very appropriate to flush the kidneys and general genito-urinary area if an infection had set in – cystitis, for instance, or water retention. Flushing may help stones or slight incontinence, either experienced by children when bed-wetting (combine with nerve teas) or often by women after childbirth. For those who are feeling sluggish, depressed, very angry or suffering from jaundice, hepatitis or indigestion, a good liver flush would be indicated.

It is hard, I think, to decide without someone else's advice whether these organs need these specific teas, so always use the teas in conjunction with the preventative teas and lots of fruit juices and water, ensuring the herbs are never over-used within the body. As the teas consist of simple general body building herbs and decongestants anyway, this is probably not a problem but any extremes are a bad thing (balance should always be pursued). In particular, strong diuretics, i.e. herbs that flush the kidneys, should not be used for any length of time, that is why the only diuretics I have used are those which are quite safely taken long term.

Some of you will notice some very common diuretic herbs to apparently be missing, like uva-ursi and juniper berries. This is the reason why: uva-ursi is a strong diuretic and strengthening to the kidneys, while juniper is extremely strong, making a very useful antiseptic for that area. Seek further advice for their excellent short-term use.

The kidneys

For the same reason as in the *Bowel building tea*, strong purgatives and laxatives have not been used as large diuretic doses could make the kidneys' action redundant. This is quite a problem with people on synthetic drug diuretics, who have started taking pills due to an oedema/weight problem, but who end up with kidney failure.

So let me start with *Kidney building tea*, the main constituent of which is dandelion, being the safest, most useful diuretic in the botanic kingdom.

The kidneys filter and excrete waste and toxic substances. When blood flows through the renal glomeruli and tubules, most of the water content and some useful substances it contains are re-absorbed into the circulation and leave behind urine.

Kidney building tea
Parts

1 Plantain (leaf)	Excellent herb for all kidney and bladder troubles.
1 Marshmallow (root)	As a demulcent, it is very soothing and healing to inflamed genito-urinary areas; it is also diuretic.
1 Ginger (root)	As a stimulant, guiding all other herbs to the right area; also calming and warming.
5 Dandelion (root)	The safest diuretic in the botanical kingdom, building the kidneys, mostly due to its high mineral content.
2 Chamomile (flower)	Soothing to the nerves, it relieves congestion and stimulates a good flow of blood.
1 Parsley (leaf)	A very ancient diuretic, it is particularly helpful for difficult or painful urination. (Do not use if there is inflammation).
1 Golden rod (leaf)	Excellent for all kidney and bladder ailments; very useful in cystitis.

A simple tea and pleasant tasting, made delicious with orange oil and orange blossom honey. *Or* squeeze the juice of half a lemon and, using 2 tsps, add to the tea and honey.

The skin

Although not often thought of as an organ, the skin is the largest organ in the body and is closely linked with the kidneys. Therefore the skin must be kept clean and in good condition, preventing dirt and toxins from entering the body and allowing toxins out through perspiration. The blood purifying tea mentioned earlier in this chapter is an excellent skin cleanser.

The liver and gall bladder

Now we shall move on to another major 'clearing house' organ – the liver – disfunctions of which cause many problems. This is perhaps the seat of most illness. As my teacher, Dr Christopher, always said, 'Show me a bad liver and I'll show you potential cancer.'

The liver has several functions, such as rendering harmless certain toxic products of the body metabolism, manufacturing and storing many nutrients (such as glucose, vitamins, etc.), storing blood, making blood and breaking down products of metabolism. As you will see, the liver is a very important organ, while the gall bladder is very closely allied to it. Due to the formation of stones caused by a faulty diet (sugar, cakes, white flour, etc.), more gall bladders are removed than any other organ in the body – the most common operation performed by western surgeons. The removal of the gall bladder makes the job of the liver all the more difficult yet more vital.

This is an excellent drink for those without a gall bladder or with malfunction of both organs. If gall stones are present, add marshmallow to the tea – in two parts for its demulcent properties.

Liver and gall bladder tea
Parts

4 Dandelion (root)	No better hepatic herb, mostly due to its mineral content. It improves digestion, influences the liver generally and stimulates secretion of bile.
1 Ginger (root)	This enhances the effectiveness of the whole tea, very helpful for indigestion, stimulating the liver in general.
1 Liquorice (rhizome)	Generally stimulative and beneficial to the liver and gall bladder.
2 Agrimony (leaf)	Excellent for all liver complaints, especially jaundice. It gives tone to the entire system and promotes the assimilation of food. It is astringent.

1 St John's wort (leaf)	The herb is astringent and soothing, greatly helping to de-toxify the liver.
1 Wild cherry (bark)	Helpful for dissolving and eliminating bile.
1 Fennel (seed)	Stimulative, yet calming; excellent for indigestion and flatulence.
1 Catnip (leaf)	Relieves pain and soothes, especially those ills associated with digestion; expels wind and gas.
1 Peppermint (leaf and flower)	As a wonderful stimulant for the liver, it is also an antispasmodic, assisting indigestion, calming and soothing. It can break down congestions and restore a functional equilibrium.
2 Parsley (root)	Excellent for treating all chronic diseases and ailments of the liver, including gall stones. (Do not use if there is inflammation present, due to its warming properties).
3 Centaury (whole herb)	For the liver, it corrects and regulates the over-secretion of bile; similar to gentian, but not quite so bitter.

A lot of liver herbs are naturally bitter and have not been included in this book due to their unpalatable taste. However, with treatment from a practitioner, these will very likely be prescribed and should be 'tasted' for the herb's full working effectiveness as the action starts with the secretion of saliva; one such herb is gentian.

The heart

Next we can look at a heart tonic and builder, useful for the entire range of heart disfunctions, for high or low blood pressure. See section on *Teas for specific ailments – of an acute nature*. **Do not use this tea for those conditions**.

The heart has a lot of work to do, mainly involving the transport of blood, but it also houses some emotional feelings and 'mental' activity. Weaknesses of the heart may show themselves in palpitations, forgetfulness, insomnia, or the constraints of valves, narrowing and blocking. As a generally supportive heart tea, this is useful if 'general weakness' is the diagnosis.

Heart building tea
Parts

2 Buckwheat (leaf)	Containing rutin, which is very strengthening to the arteries and cardiac muscles. It is an excellent nutritive as well.
2 Devil's claw (whole herb)	Rejuvenates and elasticates blood vessels. Equalises high and low blood pressure.

2 Hawthorn (berry)	Helpful to correct low blood pressure, rapid or uneven heart beat, inflammation of the muscle; also for insomnia due to heart problems; also good for varicose veins.
2 Ginseng (root)	Excellent heart and circulatory herb, normalises low blood pressure, reduces blood cholesterol.
1½ Ginger (root)	Stimulant/carminative for the circulation.
1½ Comfrey (root)	Demulcent; its mucilaginous and cell-proliferant qualities soften and rebuild arteries, muscle, etc.
1 Cayenne (pepper)	Food for the circulatory system, it feeds necessary elements into the cell structure of the arteries, veins and capillaries, so they can regain their elasticity, and blood pressure returns to normal.
2 Kelp	Restores elasticity and helps to unblock arteries.
4 Motherwort (leaf)	Excellent heart tonic, calms and supports the heart and nerves.
1 Coriander (seed)	Very strengthening to the heart; adds an interesting flavour.
1 Vervain (leaf)	Building in general for a weak heart.
2 Centaury (whole herb)	General tonic and strengthener for the heart.

Note: For high and low blood pressure. In addition a tablespoon of wheatgerm oil each day is advisable as it has the effect of toning cardiac muscle.

For those with high blood pressure, delete ginseng and liquorice, while those with low blood pressure should delete the hawthorn – add more cayenne for both conditions.

The spleen

If I were a Chinese herbalist working amongst the Chinese, beyond the liver and the kidneys I would include the spleen as a major organ. They believe this to be more important than any other organ. The spleen is responsible for transport and conversion, which includes digestion, absorption and transport of the best food nutrients, the spleen transferring these products of metabolism to all tissues and vital organs. It also regulates fluid balance in the body and controls muscles of the body's extremities – mouth, etc. – and produces fresh blood, affecting blood circulation transport.

. Deficiencies in the spleen show themselves in a distended stomach, watery stools, oedema, weight loss, dry lips, loss of appetite and poor digestion. The stomach directly affects and is affected by the spleen as it digests the food prior to the spleen's activities. This is why symptoms like post-natal distension, hiccups, vomiting and constipation may also appear.

Spleen and stomach restoration tea
Parts

5 Dandelion (root)	This stimulates the spleen activity, and is good for the stomach, liver, kidneys and pancreas.
3 Lemon balm (leaf)	Valuable aid in digestion and activation of spleen. Aids vomiting and nausea.
1 Cinnamon (bark)	Stimulating to all body organs, it is also a carminative, removing gas from the intestinal tract; excellent for stomach weakness and nausea.
½ Liquorice (rhizome)	Guide to the other herbs; it stimulates all organs.
1 Ginger (root)	As a general organ stimulant, it also removes stomach gas.
2 Allspice	Excites the activity of the stomach and, therefore, activates the spleen. It is a carminative and helpful for indigestion.
1 Sassafras (root)	This stimulates the activity of the spleen (and kidneys); helpful for stomach spasms.

Teas for specific ailments – of an acute nature

This next section deals with those ailments which manifest themselves as sudden, direct illnesses, like influenza, high fever, a bad cough, toothache, and so on. The herbs used are strong and direct, stimulating the body's natural defences. The more forceful approach is correct because the body is otherwise in a strong and fit state, therefore mild tonic herbs and dilution should be avoided. Strong, neat doses are what is required and, happily, the effect is just as rapid. 'Flu can normally last seven to fourteen days but with this method two days might be the duration. The attitude is not to suppress this illness, driving it back into the body for an apparently rapid cure, but to force the toxins out, leaving nothing for the germs to feed upon, stimulating the body's own defence mechanism. This does not mean that a short 'healing crisis' will not be experienced before a complete recovery.

However, like any illness, it is vitally important for a recuperative period, using 'tonic' herbs after the event to replace the drain on the body during the intense healing period. The *Vitamin, mineral and nutritive herbal tea*, the *Daily health tea* or the *Organ and system building teas* are appropriate here.

The design of the tea formulae for this 'acute' section returns to that of the building, daily teas, i.e. the stronger herbs in large proportion with carminative, demulcent, antispasmodic and stimulative herbs to back them up. However, where a very unbalanced condition of Yin and Yang occurs (like the next two recipes) then herbs of similar potency and nature will be used in equal proportions.

Influenza, colds and feverishness

This tea is aimed at provoking perspiration, but this kind of treatment should *only* be used if the patient is hot, has a high fever and is generally strong anyway.

All these herbs induce sweating, forcing out the toxins.

Influenza, colds and fever tisane
Parts
1 Elderflower
or
1 Peppermint (flower and leaf)
1 Catnip (leaf)
or
1 Lemon balm (leaf)
1 Yarrow (foliage)
1 Meadowsweet (leaf)

Note: This tea should be drunk strong and preferably unsweetened (although yarrow is very bitter). Follow with a hot bath and drink in the bath. Go immediately to bed with plenty of warm covers to sweat it out. Every four hours, drink two more cups of the tea. If there is excessive sweating already, include ginger and cinnamon in the tea and bath.

Low fever tea
Dandelion root ⎫
Burdock root   ⎪
Devil's claw root ⎬   Equal parts.
Motherwort   ⎪
Comfrey root   ⎭

Make a strong tea by simmering in a saucepan for 20 minutes. Take half a cup every two hours. Later on add rosehip and parsley to these teas for extra vitamin C. Meadowsweet at any time adds natural aspirin.

Note: If the patient has a low fever, weak pulse and is generally pale and debilitated, then use these herbs and follow up with the *Vitamin, mineral and nutritive herb tea* after the fever has gone in order to rebuild the body's strength. For the high fever, flowers and leaves are used to balance the Yang condition, which is strong, hot and superficial; while for low fever mostly roots have been used to penetrate the deeper organs and to balance the Yin condition (weak, cold, deep).

Coughs and sore throats

The Upper respiratory tisane would do admirably for this condition, otherwise a stronger, swifter acting tea.

103

Cough and throat tisane
Parts
2 Red raspberry (leaf)
3 Wild cherry (bark)
1 Liquorice (rhizome)
3 Coltsfoot (leaf)
1 Mullein (leaf)
1 Sage (leaf)
Check back to the *Upper respiratory tisane* for their particular benefits.

Cystitis

Now let us turn to a problem that plagues mostly women (but some men): cystitis or frequent and painful urination caused by over-sensitivity. This is an inflammation of the urinary bladder, caused usually by a bacterial infection but sometimes from mechanical irritation, e.g. crystalline deposits in the urine, a chill, etc. Urine is normally free from bacteria but it can become contaminated if the bacteria from the large intestine (which is healthy and normal there) strays to the renal pelvis via the blood. However, more likely the infection would have spread up the urethra from the bladder. The reason women are more prone to this problem than men is due to the short, badly protected outlet of the female bladder.

Another cause can be 'stagnant urine', which is liable to infection; this can be caused by pressure of some kind, preventing complete emptying of the bladder, e.g. pressure of the foetus in pregnancy, kidney stones or enlarged prostrate gland. The infection can become acute, with a high temperature and pain over the kidneys, but occasionally it becomes chronic with acute attacks at intervals over many years.

The tea is for the more common, infrequent form of cystitis which can be aggravated by frequent coffee drinking.

Cystitis tea
Parts

1 Burdock (root)	Antibiotic.
2 Golden rod (leaf)	Diuretic and strengthening to the bladder.
4 Dandelion (root)	Diuretic.
2 Agrimony (leaf)	Diuretic.
1 Echinacea (root)	Natural antibiotic.
1 Peppermint (leaf)	Acts as an antispasmodic and carminative.
1 Marshmallow (leaf)	Demulcent, softening to inflammation.

Either make a single tea: make a weak cup, e.g. 6-12g to 600ml, infuse in boiling water and drink *cold*. Or add chamomile oil to 1 tsp honey and eat off the spoon. Chamomile taken cold relieves congestions, so for any stagnation it is ideal.

Diarrhoea

During the summer months, adults and particularly children can suffer from a 'runny tummy', due to the bounty of fresh fruit. This kind of diarrhoea is easily helped with this tea. Otherwise, natural diarrhoea is nature's way of ridding toxins from the body and the signal should be listened to with a fasting period. However, diarrhoea is debilitating and this tea would greatly help its weakening effects. This tea should not be used with chronic forms of diarrhoea, where the *Bowel building tea* should be taken.

A tisane for diarrhoea
Parts

1 Mullein (leaf)	Its mucilaginous qualities help to coat and protect the bowel. It is also antispasmodic to help with any associated pain.
3 Marshmallow (leaf)	The mucilage in this herb is protective and healing to the irritations caused by diarrhoea.
1 Plantain (leaf)	This cooling, soothing herb greatly helps calm diarrhoea.
1 Nettle (leaf)	Iron content counteracts anaemia, which can cause diarrhoea.
1 Yellow dock (root)	As above.
3 Oak (bark)	Astringent and tightening, it helps strengthen.
1 Wood betony (whole herb)	Alterative and nervine, it is wonderfully effective for diarrhoea.
1 Chamomile (flower)	Binding, calming and soothing.
2 Motherwort (leaf)	Tonic for gastro-intestinal tract, helpful for debilitation or weakness with diarrhoea.
1 Comfrey (leaf)	Cell-proliferant qualities repair any damaged tissue.

Hayfever

During the summer months it need not just be diarrhoea that is prevalent but, with the pollen count up, hayfever can be rife. I suggest using the *Upper respiratory tisane* and the *Lymphatic infection tea*, but this is a special, more instant tea which would also help other true allergies.

Hayfever, allergy and irritant tea
Parts

6 Eyebright (flower and leaf)	Detoxifying, it relieves nose, eye and throat inflammation. Highly alterative.
3 Plantain (leaf)	Natural antihistamine.
6 Chickweed (leaf)	Natural antihistamine.

1 Mullein (leaf)	Relieves sinus congestion, promoting absorption of fluids.
1 Burdock (root)	Aids job of lymphatic system to decongest; also alterative.
1 Cayenne (pepper)	Stimulant.
1 Parsley (leaf)	Removes excess mucus and decongests.
1 Marshmallow (leaf)	Soothing, healing to mucus membranes.

This is so helpful for the runny nose and streaming eyes that hayfever can produce, without the sleepy effects that hayfever drugs can induce.

Flatulence

Flatulence (wind) can produce tremendous discomfort and distension. Either it can be caused by fermentation in the lower intestine caused by constipation, in which case the *Bowel building tea* and *Liver and gall bladder tea* should be used; or, air is swallowed when gulping food and drink too hastily. Slowing this process down would greatly help, but to aid discomfort and expel the air this tea is wonderfully effective.

Tisane for flatulence
Parts

3 Caraway (seed)	Aid to digestion and helpful to indigestion; also gas and cholic.
1 Catmint (catnip) (leaf)	Relaxant, diffusive, stimulant, sedative; generally helpful to whole condition.
2 Centaury (leaf)	Regulates the liver and digestion, thus relieves wind.
3 Ginger (flakes)	Relieves pain of gas; carminative.
1 Pennyroyal (leaf)	A warming influence on the stomach and stimulative for ridding gas, helping the action of the ginger.
1 Thyme (leaf)	Helpful for any foul odours and settling of the stomach.
1 Sassafras (root)	Especially helpful in the pains and spasms of acute flatulence. Excellent general cleanser of fermented foods.
	(Do not use in pregnancy; do not use for longer than three weeks.)

Toothache and bleeding gums

I used this formula to illustrate the basic structure of composing a tea combination, now I will explain its action.

Toothache tea rinse
Parts

Plantain	Stimulating and alterative to the circulatory system.
2 Chamomile (flower)	Soothing to the nerves, it is excellent for toothache and neuralgia.
3 Hop (flower)	Powerful, stimulating and relaxing nerve tonic; increases capillary action, helps relieve pain.
1 Cloves	Antispasmodic, increases circulation; is rubefacient, balancing out local pain.
1 Meadowsweet (leaf)	Carminative, demulcent and anodyne.
1 Cayenne (pepper)	Activates the carminative to greater use; equalises blood pressure, reducing centralised pressure, causing pain.

Note: Rather than drinking this, make as a tea, even stronger than normal, i.e. simmer in a saucepan for 20 minutes, and rinse round the mouth as often as possible.

While we are still on the subject of teeth, let me give you a recipe, again to rinse with, rather than drink, for bleeding gums.

Bleeding gum rinse
Parts

1 Echinacea (root)	Comforting and stimulating antiseptic; anti-bacterial.
3 Cayenne (pepper)	Blood equaliser, arrests bleeding almost instantaneously.
3 Oak (bark)	Tannin content makes it astringent, contracting gums; helps soreness.
1 Sage (leaf)	Astringent, healing antiseptic.
1 Thyme (leaf)	Healing antiseptic.
2 Red raspberry (leaf)	Excellent for gargle or mouth wash.

Proper dental care will prevent bleeding gums, e.g. regular brushing/ massage of the gums and teeth – use tincture of myrrh – including, of course, general body maintenance. A gum disorder could also be a sign of calcium deficiency, so the *Vitamin, mineral and nutritive herbal tea* would help. It is also a sign of strain or stress or general body debility.

Dandruff

Another ailment that often goes with bleeding gums is dandruff and sudden hair loss, so for these drink either the *Daily health tea, Vitamin, mineral and nutritive herbal tea* or the *Sleep and nerve tonic tea.*

Headaches and indigestion

For headaches, the recipe for *Migraine tea* is excellent, while indigestion is best dealt with by taking the *Liver and gall bladder tea* – of course, indigestion can cause headaches. Alternatively, a quick tea can be made up of peppermint, aniseed and dill.

Loss of appetite

Also connected with liver disfunction is the condition of appetite loss, due to lack of gastric juice secretions, so here is a special tea.

Appetite loss tea
Parts

2 Blessed thistle (leaf)	Increases gastric and bile secretion.
1 Marigold (flower)	Promotes bile secretion.
2 Cinnamon (flakes)	Stimulates secretion of gastric juices.
4 Dandelion (root)	Stimulates bile, gastric juices and pancreas; a general liver tonic.
1 Echinacea (root)	General appetite inducer; stomach tonic.
1 Ginger (root) 1 Thyme (leaf)	Both help generally with loss of appetite.

Slimming

Rather opposite to appetite loss is the need to lose weight and here is an excellent tea which corrects this problem safely and gradually, without robbing the body of important nutrients. Weight loss is important to relieve many other conditions, i.e. heart strain.

Weight loss, slimming tisane
Parts

2 Kelp	Feeds the thyroid and other malfunctioning glands, gains healthier state for holding weight control. Activates metabolism.
2 Chickweed (leaf)	Reduces excess fat, being a mild diuretic and laxative. Nutritive, important for relief of nervous system due to dieting.
2 Burdock (root)	Excellent diuretic and blood purifier, and eliminates excess nervous energy, possibly caused by dieting.
1 Liquorice (rhizome)	Stimulative, aiding rest of formula, generally activating sluggishness of the system, especially the liver.
1 Fennel (leaf or seed)	Antispasmodic, carminative and stimulant, all vital to help formula work; also a diuretic.

2 Dandelion (root)	Active, safe diuretic, and liver and spleen stimulant. Also helps poor blood system levels, causing weight gain.
1 Echinacea (root)	Activates general elimination, good blood purifier.
2 Golden rod (leaf)	Helps regenerate kidney activity; poor kidney action causes water retention.
2 Parsley (root)	Excellent diuretic.

Note: Use extra kelp tablets. If also hypoglycaemic, use extra dandelion.

The menstrual cycle

A surprising number of women suffer from menstrual disorders of some kind or another. They can be caused by unbalanced hormone levels, bad diet, local shock, emotion or stress. As there are so many kinds of menstrual problems, I have started with a general tea and then two more specific ones.

Pain, menstrual cramps, irregularity and fluid balance tea

Parts

1 Horsetail (foliage)	Calcium and silica; also diuretic.
1 Nettle (leaf)	High in iron; ensures calcium assimilation.
1 Chamomile (flower)	Analgesic in action, helping pain.
2 Ginger (root)	Excellent for cramps and nausea.
1 Dandelion	Increases flow of urine, decreases blood pressure and purifies blood. High in easily assimilated calcium.
1 Raspberry (leaf)	Regulates and reduces menstrual cramps. High in iron.
2 Marjoram (leaf)	Excellent for menstrual cramps and nausea.
1 Blessed thistle (foliage)	Allays pain and helps cramps. High in calcium.
1 Pennyroyal (leaf)	Important in the regulation of menstrual flow and for relieving cramps.
1 Sarsaparilla (root)	Rich in hormones which help to balance hormone levels.
1 Thyme (leaf)	Anaesthetic, nervine sedative, helpful for cramps and pains.
1 Motherwort (foliage)	Helpful for spasms, tones uterine membrane.

Excessive menstrual flow tea

Parts

| 1 Yarrow (leaf) | Stops excessive menstrual bleeding due to astringent qualities; helps cramps. |

109

1 Plantain (leaf)	Cooling, soothing properties help excessive menstrual flow.
1 Red raspberry (leaf)	Decreasing menstrual flow without abrupt action.
1 Cayenne (pepper)	Regulates blood flow by toning arteries' capillaries, etc; stops excessive bleeding.

Note: A bitter tea! Drink with fruit juice concentrate.

Delayed or obstructed menstruation – amenorrhoea tea
Parts

1 Horehound (leaf)	Promotes gentle outward flow of the blood.
1 Peppermint (leaf)	Breaks down congestions and equalises circulation.
1 Thyme (leaf)	Helpful for cramps and pain.
1 Pennyroyal (leaf)	In inflammatory congestion and obstruction, this herb raises body temperature, relaxes spasms and stimulates the blood throughout.
½ Ginger (root)	Stimulates blood throughout.
1 Wood betony (foliage)	Calming and soothing for emotional suppression.
1 Motherwort (leaf)	Promotes flow of menses, helpful to emotional nervous suppression.

Teas for specific ailments – of a chronic nature

Having started this chapter by saying that too much time is spent in observations of symptoms on diagnosis and naming of specific ailments, I did relent a little and concede that attention could be paid to symptoms and ailments as long as the whole picture had been carefully observed.

Over many years now and for many hundreds of people – tea drinkers and sufferers – I have some standard tea recipies. These are for people with very common problems like arthritis, rheumatism, insomnia, etc. Their health has been greatly improved, if not cured, with these standard teas, alongside diet, exercise and mental enhancement.

All the herb teas in this section could be described as treatments for chronic ailments, i.e. diseases or illnesses which are long term and where many organ systems have been affected. The approach with these teas for these conditions should be slow and gentle and a very gradual change should be looked for, as chronic illness causes debilitation and the energy of the sufferer is very low. Strong symptoms resulting from the drinking of the tea are not a good sign and less should be taken or the tea changed in subtle ways. Slowly the chronic disease will hopefully get to the point where it manifests itself as an 'acute disease' – think of it as water, very,

very slowly coming to the boil. For this reason the tea formulas take a different form, having no strong herbs in large proportions. This is a healthy sign but this point should never be rushed – it is often so-called 'unpleasant' and the correct term for it is a 'healing crisis', where an acute mirroring of the ailment is seen. During the time, toxins are being eliminated very rapidly and at this time stronger herbs may be used with more direct effect.

Again, consult someone in the practice of natural healing if your own instincts or knowledge is scanty, as treating this moment in the correct way is critical. This healing crisis stage is an important point in the healing process and can make all the difference between complete recovery or a return to the old condition. One herb which should always be included is liquorice, which acts as a balance to the formula, avoiding any bad side effects; the Chinese call it 'the peacemaker', though in cases of high blood pressure it can exacerbate the condition. However, the proportions of it are always rather small.

Arthritis and rheumatism
Normally the prerogative of the elderly, arthritis does, very occasionally, strike out at children but only roughly one in a thousand at present. There are many forms of arthritis and rheumatism but there is a rough generalisation about them all, mostly that they cause pain. Drinking this tea will do a great deal to help the problem and the pain. With the correct diet, attitude to life and stress and some exercises, the condition may even go away but, even so, this herb tea will cause a stabilisation to occur. In other words, the condition may get no worse but neither will much improvement be made, because as quickly as the herb tea is flushing out toxins, acids and feeding the body with necessary vitamins and minerals, the *cause* of the condition still goes on unchanged. Let me explain some of the causes of these two painful problems: arthritis and rheumatism.

Stress is a major cause of many illnesses, and in the case of arthritis and rheumatism the same applies. This doesn't just mean a stressful situation, it means how people measure up to, or cope with, stress. Stress means that the body itself is under attack, causing us to react to certain things in differing ways. Most of our diet today causes continual stress, a lot of us are on 'red alert' most of the day – we may not appear this way to outsiders, however, as some of us have become adept at hiding it. For instance, white sugar (or any sugar for that matter) plunges straight into the bloodstream, raising the blood sugar level very fast – this sugar rush causes hyperactivity, and for what? We are on red alert with nothing to do, our adrenalin is rushing and the situation really doesn't merit the body's response. Our reaction, therefore, could be anger, fear, temper, or whatever. The same sort of thing happens when we constantly take stimulants like tea, coffee and salt. We are 'hyped up' – with no where to go. Is it surprising that our behaviour is unbalanced? Of course there are many physical reactions – for instance, calcium is stripped from our bones for nerve and muscle use. Blood pressure rises so that oxygen, sugar and calcium can travel more quickly to the tissues and this highly protective stress reaction becomes abused and over-used; 'crying wolf' would be an apt expression.

In normal and very occasional stress situations the body is equipped to rebuild after the 'adrenalin event', repairing cell damage, returning blood pressure to normal and replacing lost calcium and all the other necessary vitamins, minerals, proteins, fats and carbohydrates for normal bodily functions. But what if our nutrition levels are totally inadequate to meet these demands through constant over-use? Our pancreas becomes 'trigger-happy' with all the sugar abuse, causing low blood sugar. Our adrenal hormones become worn out, adrenalin ceases to be released and generally our resistance is lowered.

An invasion is inevitable with any kind of disease likely to enter our system; arthritis and rheumatism being just two. Here the removal of calcium from the bones to be deposited into the arteries, tissue, muscle and joints will be familiar to many sufferers for the pain it causes. The manufacturing of calcium within the body is reliant on vitamin D, available from sunshine and oily fish, especially cod-liver oil. Therefore, this is one place to start. There should also be sufficient potassium intake found in potato peelings and bananas – plus iodine with daily kelp tablets, and natural calcium also contained in the latter.

Another factor concerning calcium is the alkaline/acid ratio within the body; acid foods like coffee, eggs, marmalade and toast (a typical breakfast) use up calcium and other minerals, trying to restore an alkaline balance. Storage of toxins, ureic acid, insufficient calcium and calcium deposits all go towards the familiar inflammation, stiffness and aching.

The whole picture, therefore, points to a mental and emotional change, plus dietary changes with correct nutritional input – the herbs seek to do the latter, whilst cleansing and healing. In fact, correct feeding can and does change mental and emotional attitudes. With children the change is very fast, with adults after many years of damage this can take longer, and help in the way of meditation – yoga or just a restful and enjoyable hobby – can speed the process. You may have been born with a tendency or hereditary weakness towards a particular illness but it does not mean you have to succumb to it.

Arthritis and rheumatism herb tea
Parts
½ Cayenne (pepper)　　Equalises any blood pressure problems.

2 Nettles (leaf)	Ensures intake of calcium into the body; high in iron, potassium and protein.
2 Dandelion (root)	Extremely safe diuretic, able to flush out toxins. High in natural and easily assimilable minerals.
1 St John's wort (leaf)	Cleansing to the liver, de-toxifies, heals and restores tissue, muscle and cells.
1 Meadowsweet (leaf)	Acts as a natural 'aspirin' to help with pain. As a very mucilaginous plant it coats and softens inflamed joints. It is also a diuretic, removing acid build-ups.
½ Liquorice (rhizome)	'The peacemaker'.
1 Burdock (root)	Excellent blood purifier and rich in natural hormones, which assist the adrenals.
1 Comfrey (root)	Important for cell repair and protein content. Helpful for inflammation.
1 Horsetail (all foliage)	Strong diuretic, for removing toxins, acids, etc. High in calcium and silica.
1 Scullcap (all foliage)	Rebuilds nervous system which is worn due to lack of calcium, helps pain level by calming the whole body.
1 Sarsaparilla (root)	Excellent blood purifier, contains natural hormones, helpful to adrenals, especially cortin. Contains potassium and is a diuretic.

Any of the essential oils can be added to this tea but lemon, peppermint or orange are the most pleasant with this one; it even tastes nice unadorned.

Using one desertspoonful to a mugful of boiling water (25g to 600ml), take this tea four to five times a day, six days a week, changing to the *Vitamin, mineral and nutrative herbal tea* on the seventh day, or just concentrated apple juice.

Stress, hyperactivity, lack of sleep and insomnia

These are all pretty much the same thing and if you have never been a poor sleeper in general then you must have had the odd night when you have woken in the early hours of the morning unable to return to sleep. Six or seven o'clock finally arrives and you feel exhausted, crumpled and frustrated, your mind has been tossing and turning, just like your body, for hours. The nasty trick that is often played on these sufferers, who are true insomniacs, is that just as sheer exhaustion pushes them to drift off to sleep at seven o'clock the alarm bell rings and rise they must, to struggle off to work. Often these people have taken sleeping pills but the body no longer responds to this sledgehammer effect unless, or course, stronger doses are then administered.

I have already discussed stress and hyperactivity and you will now realise that without proper diet and mental adjustment a frayed nervous system is inevitable. Lack of calcium is a major factor as this sheaths the nerve endings and without this protection they rub like live wires, causing untold strain and stress. Lack of sleep itself is harmful to the body as sleep is our natural way of healing, mending, resting and restoring the body for another day's activity. The first four hours of *undisturbed* sleep are the most important in the whole night, therefore if just this pattern can be established at the beginning then things are looking up.

The nervous system in general controls coordination and synergistic activities of all organs of the human body. It should provide correct reactions to environmental stimuli in order to maintain balance, mentally and physically.

Sleep and nerve tonic tea
All equal parts

Scullcap (all foliage)	A safe, reliable nerve sedative, it feeds, regulates, strengthens and rehabilitates the nerve cells, particularly re-sheathing the nerve endings. It stimulates the production of nerve fluid yet calms; its healing is permanent. Slow working, it should be taken regularly over a long period of time.
Wood betony (leaf)	A nerve tonic and sedative, it also cleanses impurities from the blood, liver and spleen.
Elderflower	Alterative and stimulant, it will quickly remove toxins affecting blood circulation, lungs, bowels and skin.
Hop (flower)	A powerful, stimulating, relaxing nerve tonic. Hops help relieve pain and have many beneficial actions in all organs and channels.
Vervain (leaf)	Excellent in any nervous conditions, it also induces sweating in bed, ridding the body of toxins.
Horsetail (all foliage)	High in calcium and silica, to furbish the nervous system.
Lime tree (flower)	Always use freshly dried leaves as old ones produce narcotic intoxication.
Passion flower	As a sedative this effectively quietens the nervous system as well as rebuilding it.
Chamomile (flower)	Calming and soothing to the entire nervous system; sedative in action.
Comfrey (root)	Rich in B vitamins, vital for feeding of nervous system.

Lemon balm (leaf)	Treatment of nervous disorders; in general soothing and calming.
Nettle (leaf)	Help assimilate the calcium, and provide other vitamins and minerals.
½ Cayenne (pepper)	This leads the herbs in, stimulating and enhancing their activities.
½ Liquorice (rhizome)	'The peacemaker'.

Note: Include burdock (root) if excessive nervous energy is present, while zinc should be included in the diet, i.e. whole grains, Brewers' yeast, and seed sprouts – the latter also giving B vitamins.

This tea can be drunk at the normal strength either as an evening or night-time drink; one to three cups while having another tea during the day, or fruit juices. Or if the person is chronic and the illness deep-seated, then it can be drunk all day, approximately five cups, according to the sufferer's body weight.

This is a very helpful tea for those people who are on sleeping tablets or tranquillisers and wish to wean themselves off them (with their doctors' help) as the effect of the herbs will match the effect of the drugs. Always reduce the drugs gradually.

Relaxing, deep sleep tea
Parts

3 Kava-kava (root)	As a nervine, it is also antispasmodic; an analgesic, antiseptic, sedative, tonic and diuretic.
2 Lime tree (flower)	As before.
2 Lemon balm (leaf)	As before.
1 Liquorice (rhizome)	'The peacemaker'.
1 Hop (flower)	As before.

Note: This tea is to be used in cases of intermittent sleeping problems only, but **not for long-term sleeping difficulties**, which should be treated with the previous tea.

It is very useful in cases where the problem is due to an upset body, giving a speedy, restful sleep – for example, in the case of jet lag or shift work. It is particularly useful when only a few hours' sleep are possible; it does, however, sometimes produce clear, epic-length dreams!

Ulcers

So many people seem to suffer from ulcers, due to poor digestion and assimilation of excess acid (duodenal ulcers), all due to a poor diet. Much of this is, of course, due to stress and, sadly, ulcerative conditions and similar illness are a common modern problem. Heartburn, nausea, stomach distention and occasional anaemia and internal bleeding are some of the symptoms.

115

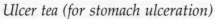

Ulcer tea (for stomach ulceration)
Parts

1 Aloe vera (foliage)	Extremely healing to ulcers; however, according to which parts of the plant used it can be a laxative and cause griping, so always combine with ginger. Otherwise use Aloe vera juice.
1 Ginger (root)	Helps griping pain of aloe; excellent for bleeding and anaemia.
1 Nettle (leaf)	Excellent for bleeding and anaemia.
1 Comfrey (root)	Aids cell proliferation, healing stomach wall linings, etc. Helpful to bleeding; soothes generally. Highly nutritious.
1 Marshmallow (root)	Soothing and healing to the mucus membrane; softens and coats stomach lining to protect from abrasions of food fibre.
1 Meadowsweet (leaf)	Acts as a natural 'aspirin' to help with pain. As a very mucilaginous plant it coats and softens. The diuretic action helps remove acids.
1 Red raspberry (leaf)	Mucilaginous qualities, coats and protects stomach lining. Astringent qualities helps any bleeding; while iron and blood building qualities help anaemia.
½ Liquorice (rhizome)	Directs, stimulates and balances other herbs. Promotes healing of gastric ulcers.
½ Cayenne (pepper)	Heals ulcerations; stops any internal bleeding and re-conditions tissue.
½ Oak (bark)	Astringent action helps any internal bleeding.
1 Plantain (leaf)	Neutralises stomach acids and normalises all stomach secretions.
1 Scullcap (foliage)	Calms the system, reducing stress and excessive production of acids.
1 Dandelion (root)	Helps counteract stomach acidity by activating liver and bile.

The pancreas, hypoglycaemia and diabetes

The pancreas (and affiliated glands) can malfunction due to high or low blood sugar levels, i.e. diabetes or hypoglycaemia. This tea will even help those who are heavy insulin users, while progress can be safely monitored with glucose tolerance tests. I would also suggest Dr Christopher's herbal capsule for this problem – see his book, *Childhood Diseases*.

So many people seem to have problems of excess sugar levels, due to today's junk food direction. This tea is designed to strengthen and regulate the endocrine gland, apart from general building and balancing.

We have already discussed sugar abuse at some length but there is a state when excess sugar has been consumed over such a long period of time that the 'trigger happy' pancreas causes almost constant low blood sugar: the feeling of sluggishness and low vitality, hypoglycaemia. Many people suffer from this without realising it; they just feel depressed and low.

This tea is, in the main, an aid for the pancreas which, if deficient, causes high and low blood sugar levels. A glucose tolerance test will test for results after drinking this tea (for at least six months). Sugars must, of course, be eliminated from diet and eating should take place every two and a half hours due to debilitation.

Pancreas, companion glands, hypoglycaemia and diabetes tisane
Parts

2 Ginseng	Stimulative, rebuilding and excellent for fatigue caused by this condition. Helps pancreas regulate blood sugar levels.
2 Comfrey (root)	Helps pancreas regulate blood sugar levels.
2 Burdock (root)	Eliminates excessive nervous energy – often symptom of hypoglycaemia and a 'trigger happy' pancreas.
1 Cayenne (pepper)	Excellent anti-crisis herb; stimulant.
2 Liquorice (rhizome)	Natural sweetener due to glyceric acid, which is fifty times sweeter than cane sugar. Increases flow of saliva and pancreas function.
2 Mullein (leaf)	Generally excellent lymphatic and glandular pancreas cleanser.
2 Dandelion (root)	Excellent for pancreas rejuvenation for both hypoglycaemia and diabetes (poor blood sugar levels).
1 Kelp	Magnesium (and other vitamins and minerals), vital for the pancreas function.

Note: This tea may well help the condition of **thrush**, caused by excess sugar levels.

Thrush is not usually a chronic disease (although it can be), but rather acute. However, it is extremely unpleasant and irritating and can be caused by, or made worse by, a disturbed pancreas. This is because fungus loves sugar, feeding and multiplying on it – another reason to cut out sugar.

Migraine

Chronic migraine is a common problem for so many people today, but its origins and causes are very diverse, likewise their treatment. (These may be as diverse as overactivity of substances affecting the relaxation and contraction of arteries.) However, diet, of course, has a major importance, cleansing of the bowels is vital and stress levels or emotional upset can have great bearing on the problem. So the tea I have made deals in a very gentle way with whatever type of migraine is suffered, from whatever origin.

Migraine tea
Parts

1 Plantain (leaf)	An antihistamine, counteracting any allergic reactions.
¼ Cayenne (pepper)	Gives elasticity to blood vessels, balancing blood vessels.
1 Chamomile (flower)	Calming, soothing; helps with any nausea.
1 Rosemary (flower and leaf)	Stimulates bloodstream, dilating blood vessels.
1 Scullcap (foliage)	Sedative and calming to nervous, emotional excitement.
1 Dandelion (root)	Toxin flusher for both liver and kidneys.
1 Meadowsweet (leaf)	Helpful for pain associated with this condition.

Note: If effects are made worse by taking this tea, delete rosemary and replace with cayenne.

I would suggest the *Bowel building tea* if constipation is experienced or the *Kidney building tea* or *Liver and gall bladder tea* if those functions are suspected to be sluggish. Or for emotional, stress problems, see the *Sleep and nerve tonic tea*.

Natural beautifiers

Leaving the drinking of herbal beverages behind us for now, let us turn to some of their other uses. Further diluted they can perfume your bath; they can provide restoration for aching feet in the form of foot baths; or relieve flagging spirits and headaches in the form of waters and 'dab-ons'. Their beautifying properties – for colouring and conditioning hair and toning the skin – are legion.

All these recipes are useful for men and women.

Soakers and soothers

Perhaps a perfect recipe would be one that combined relaxation of the mind, released tense muscles and toned the skin, leaving it fresh, clean and taut. Try this recipe after a tiring day.

Relaxation bath

12g Vervain (leaf)	Soothing and pacifying, relieving tense muscles.

12g Lemon balm (leaf)	Calming and soothing to the brain and body; also very cleansing.
12g Chamomile (flower)	Calming, sedating and tranquillising.
12g Marshmallow (leaf)	Soothing and softening to the skin; prevents any itchiness.

Take the herbs and infuse in 900ml pints of water. Let it stand (covered) for a few hours before use. Run the bath, then wallow in it. Dip a flannel in the tea (a hot flannel) and then place it (now warm) on your brow – add the rest of the infusion to the bath and then lie back and close your eyes. Tensions will just slip away.

Valerian bath

A more potently soothing and tranquillising bath infusion can be made using valerian (from which valium used to be extracted and made). However, this herb, although magnificent for relieving stress and exhaustion (even hyperactivity) does smell revolting due to its valerianic acid content. Combine with lemon grass essential oil – the smell will be greatly reduced.

Parts

4 Valerian (root)	Almost sedative, extremely calming.
12 Lime tree flowers	Tranquillising and calming.
Essential oil of lemon grass	

Take 100g herb with three drops of lemon grass oil and place in a muslin bag. Drop into the bath while running in the hot water. Keep the door closed while doing this and 'drink in' the fumes. (Skin brush prior to this to allow maximum penetration of vapours.) However, always tell someone when doing this because of the very strong effect sometimes producing rapid sleepiness.

Such baths were more commonplace in centuries past than nowadays, but they are very much under-used and under-enjoyed. Whether listening to music or watching the television, it is a lovely way to relax.

Hot foot and hand bath

On a cold day or if suffering from poor circulation there is nothing more delightful than 'gingering up' the feet with stimulating herbs and, in turn, stimulating the whole body by activating all the acupressure points used in foot reflexology. Chilblains dare not appear using this mixture!

Parts

½ Cayenne (pepper)	Equalizes blood circulation; gentle stimulant.
2 Mustard (seed)	An ancient bath addition especially for those with gout, rheumatism and arthritis.

| 2 Lavender (flower) | General circulatory herb, as well as being a nervine; calming to the whole system. |

This mixture can easily be applied as a hand bath, with cold hands.

Cold foot and hand bath
There is nothing nicer than after a hot day's shopping or a hike up the mountains in climbing boots, than to slip your feet into a cooling, relaxing infusion. Hot, puffy hands are also immediately cooled and refreshed.

Parts

2 Elderflower	Cooling, detoxifying, blood purifying and thinning.
1 Chamomile (flower)	Soothing, calming.
½ Thyme (flower)	Natural deodorant.

Place a couple of grammes of herb into the bowl either loose or tied in a muslin bag and pour on the hot water first, adding the cold water last. Soak your hands or feet for five to ten minutes and finish off with cold water for 30 seconds to close pores and increase circulation.

Face steam
Notes: Asthmatics or those with heat trouble should not attempt this.
For cleansing and toning the skin there is perhaps no better method than steaming the face with hot, herby water. Toning is performed by stimulating the circulation and getting the blood up to the surface of the skin, which will help to nourish it while clogged pores are opened. The method is very simple.

Clean the face and leave the skin moist. Then take two heaped tablespoons of dried herbs and pour over 2 litres of boiling water. Stir in well. Hold your face no nearer than a ruler's length away from the water (more sensitive skin may need to be slightly further away) and keep your eyes closed. Wearing a bath hat stops hair flopping into the face while doing this. Leave your head over the basin with or without the addition of a cotton towel (for a sauna effect) until the water has cooled down. All pores will be deeply cleansed at the end of the treatment and toxins eliminated, by raising the perspiration level. Also the skin will be hydrated by adding moisture.

A general all-round herb for a face steam is comfrey, while . . .

For oily skin	Add yarrow and lavender.
For combination skin	Add marshmallow and houseleek.
For dry skin	Add meadowsweet and rose petals.
For normal skin	Add lemon balm and apple mint.

Rosemary and elderflower toner and rejuvenator
After steaming your face and opening up the pores it is then important to close them. The following is good for sensitive skin.
50g Rosemary (leaf)
50g Elderflower
12g Yarrow (leaf)
25g Rose petals
Bruise herbs in a pestle and mortar before pouring on warm water. Infuse for 20 minutes. Make an infusion 25g to 600ml of distilled water and allow to cool. Add two drops of essential oil of oranges and a dash of glycerine, well shaken. Wipe over the face twice daily.

Troubled skin cleanser and toner
For more troubled skin, that is oily and disturbed, then something more potent and balancing to the sebaceous glands is needed.
Equal parts
Witch hazel (leaf)
Yarrow (leaf)
Marshmallow (leaf)
Chickweed (leaf)
Dash cider vinegar
Take 50g herb to 1.2 litres, and make an infusion – add the cider vinegar. This can be stored in the fridge for up to three days. Use with cotton wool two to three times daily.

Hair conditioners
We now turn away from our skin to our hair. Using herbs and water again, we can make use of some natural hair tonics.

Dark hair reviver
Equal parts
Walnut (leaf)
Elderberries
Sage (leaf)
Rosemary (leaf)
Alfalfa (leaf)
Marshmallow (leaf or root)
Take 50g of herb to 1.2 litres of water, simmer for 20 minutes, reducing the water and leave to macerate for three hours. Strain off liquid and combine with shampoo on last wash. Leave on for as long as possible. Rinse off with plain hot water giving three rinses or more. It will leave the hair silky, full-bodied and healthy-looking if not colour heightened.

Light hair reviver
Parts
2 Chamomile (flower)
1 Nettle (leaf)
1 Fenugreek (seed)
1 Marshmallow (flower)
Dash lemon juice
Follow the method for *Dark hair reviver*.

Eye coolers
For tired, irritated or puffy eyes this provides almost instant relief.

Eye wash

50g Golden seal	A traditional herb for any eye ointment or eyewash.
50g Chamomile	Soothing, calming and relaxing to the eye; its essential oil is particularly refreshing.
50g Eyebright	An ancient eye herb and antihistamine.
25g Plantain	Softening and soothing to the eye and antihistamine.

Make as tea, 25g to 600ml of water. Using an eyebath this can be put into the eye as often as necessary. Can be stored for up to three days in the refrigerator.

A last word
There should be a tea for most people's problems somewhere amongst this chapter. But remember that the tea is not the whole story to healing; diet and exercise and the use of other herbs not included in this book are all important, coupled with other forms of natural healing such as acupuncture, massage, osteopathy, etc.

chapter seven

The flavour of herbs
Herbal recipes old and new

Before tea and coffee reached these Isles, wine, beer and cider (originally made from crab apple) were our main beverages, the rich drinking fine wines from France, while the poor brewed their own concoctions in their back yards, using vegetables, roots and fruits of the countryside.

Beyond this, plants were simply placed in boiling water for a herbal tea, and flavour depended on local countryside and flora. The same practice goes on, and went on, worldwide. Some herbs have become more famous than others, standing the test of taste and time, but all were originally born from simple country folk, monks, gypsies, soldiers on foot, and the like.

Old combinations

One such tea illustrates this story well.

Moorland tea

This piece of Scottish heritage, handed down by many generations, tells us many things: firstly, that all the plants used grew in profusion (and, in some areas, probably still do); and, secondly, that it was undoubtedly an ordinary, everyday tea as the recipe does not rely on fruits or flowers, just the leaves – and with many of these plants, that could mean all the year, except for when the snow covered them.

I feel sure that this tea was mainly drunk because it contained the local plants of the people who made the recipe, and it tasted nice. Also its medicinal benefits merely brought an added bonus. However, its highly antiseptic, deodorant properties were probably very useful in those days.

All equal parts

Heather flowers or heather (leaf tops)	Antiseptic and diuretic.
Bramble (leaf)	Mucilaginous and astringent.
Bilberry (leaf)	Vitamins and minerals.
Speedwell (leaf)	Astringent and bitter tonic; alterative and upper respiratory.
Wild thyme (leaf)	Antiseptic; natural deodorant.
Wild strawberry (leaf)	Vitamins and minerals.

Make as for normal tea and add heather honey if desired.

Age-old herbs and wild flowers

Often drinks made from flowers were single teas due to differing flowering periods. Honeysuckle tea (*lonicera periclymenum*) was naturally sweet; goosegrass or cleaver's tea (*galium aparine*) was soothing and sleep-inducing; gorse blossom tea (*ulex europaeus*) and primrose tea (*primula vulgaris*) were apparently helpful for gout and rheumatism; rose petal tea (*rosa canina* or any other hedgerow rose) and speedwell leaves and flowers (*veronica chamaedrys*) were tonics and astringent; and woodruff (*galium odoratum*) was good for nerves and insomnia.

Here are some more period recipes.

Seventeenth century herb tea
Parts
1 Rosemary (leaf)
2 Lemon balm (leaf)
6 Rose (leaf)
A handful of rose petals
Chop finely (once dried), and make as normal.

Eighteenth century sage tea
A handful of sage (leaf)
A handful of lemon balm (leaf)
Put both into a pan, slice in lemon peel, some honey and a glass of white wine. Pour on to this three quarts of boiling water, cover and remove herbs while cooling.

Nineteenth century balm tea
12 Sprigs of lemon balm (leaf)
6 Cloves
Juice of half a lemon
Infuse these in 600ml of boiling water for one hour, then drink as desired.

Nineteenth century herb tea
Parts
1 Agrimony (leaf)
1 Tormentil (leaf)
1 Wild marjoram (leaf)
¼ Red roses (flower)
¼ Cowslip (flower)
¼ Blackcurrant (leaf)
Chop all the above and mix well. Using a heaped tablespoon for two people, make as normal.

Another nineteenth century herb tea
Parts
11 Hawthorn (leaf)
1 Sage (leaf)
1 Balm (leaf)
Prepare as above.

Lemonades
Often, one or two herbs would be put together with the addition of lemon, which was a favourite flavouring – these were then called lemonades.

Woodsorrel and balm lemonade
2 Sprigs of lemon balm (leaf) ⎫
1 Sprig of woodsorrel (leaf) ⎬ Pickle, wash and dry.
Place in a stone jug, slice up a lemon (peeled) and add (zest off some of the peel and add also), then pour on 1.8 litres of boiling water. Add some honey and leave to cool.

Pink lemonade
The mountain ash tree, familiar to the rocky outcrops of Wales, Scotland and Cumbria, produces a 'pink lemonade', made from the ripe, red berries of any sorbus species.

Wash one cup of crushed ripe berries. Soak them in three cups of cold water for one to two hours. Strain and add honey to taste. Pour into tall glasses or over ice-cubes and garnish with a few fresh berries.

Delightful and most refreshing!

Lemon barley
This drink reminds me of my childhood. Hailing traditionally from Scotland, however, barley is common all over Britain, used in thickening soups and stews.

To make the barley water, one uses the common barley (*hordeum murinum*), using 125g to 600ml water. Boil this slightly and strain off. Replace with fresh water to give a good colour. (However, if nutrition and not colour is sought, then do not pour off the original water.) Boil this down by half and add lemon peel and honey.

To this can be added to 600ml of the drink a quarter of liquorice root (shredded), and some raisins.

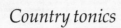

Country tonics

In those parts of the country where broom (usually sand and heath) abounds, recipes for broom flower tea may well be in the family. Still used today, there is an old 'tonic' recipe, comprising largely of this flower. The tea's tonic qualities rely on its strong diuretic action to remove toxins and acids, along with the dandelion's mineral content.

Broom tonic
25g Broom tops and flowers
12g Dandelion root or leaves
12g Bruised juniper berries
Pinch of cayenne
Boil the broom and dandelion in 600ml water until reduced by half, add the juniper berries towards the end. Strain when cool; add a pinch of cayenne and drink.

Dandelion and burdock tonic
The most famous tonic partnership of all, taken on holiday outings, into hay-making fields, down the mines, up the valleys and still drunk and made today, especially in the north. It ranks probably highest as a herbal duo. Not surprisingly so either, due to its multitude of therapeutic properties. It is still used constantly in almost every herbal formulation by modern herbalists. Use the herbs (root) in equal quantities either making a normal infusion or a decoction.

Nettle and chickweed tonic
Again, two famous partners and, made into a tea using equal parts, there is no better and easier fresh, free tonic. The nettles are best picked very young, tender and green, while the chickweed is best plucked when it grows lush and succulent. Nettles should never be picked beyond June as their chemical constituents change, to produce a laxative herb! Anyway, they lose their flavour and become rather stringy. So always remember to harvest for the year in springtime.

Birch and sorrel tonic
Vitamin packed, diuretic and tasty, this spring tonic is a very old favourite and traditionally drunk over Easter.

Groundsel and ground ivy tonic (Senecio vulgaris)
Two very common weeds/herbs and both packed with vitamins, minerals; general diuretic, blood purifying properties. Ground ivy was made as a single tea, known as 'gill tea', sold in the 'cries' of London.

Primrose, violet and cowslip tea
These pretty little flowers were once made into teas, wines and cordials, but their scarcity has made that impossible now. Their abundant vitamin content and general tonic properties made them an invaluable tea, and they were frequently used when children refused other foods and drinks as they were pretty and fun to pick.

Oddity teas

Seed teas; not strictly teas, but not strictly anything else!

Sunflower seed tea
Boil the seed and simmer for 20 minutes. The liquor can be used as cough medicine with honey added and a sprig of sage.

Rice tea
(The Japanese often mix rice with their green teas.)
Often used in the days of nannies and nursery teas. This was used when, quite rightly so, tea (Indian) was considered too strong. The rice was browned in the oven and then made as an ordinary tea infusion.

Psyllum seed tea
A softening seed that swells on absorption. It absorbs water from the gut and is, therefore, helpful for the bowels.

Celery seed tea
Parts
9 Celery (seed)
2 Lemon balm
Drop of juniper oil
Infuse as normal, adding honey if desired. Celery is an excellent diuretic, tonic and nutritive, making this tea useful for any water retention problems; also for rheumatism and arthritis.

Linseed tea
Parts
1 Linseed
½ Liquorice (shredded)
Zest of lemon rind
1 litre Water
Honey to taste
Boil the linseed and lemon peel zest in the water, then simmer for 30 minutes, finally adding other ingredients. Drink when cool.

Sesame seed tea
25g Sesame (seed)
600ml Boiling water
A strong tasting honey is needed. Infuse as normal. This is ideal for children, with its fairly bland flavour, easily pepped up with fruit juice concentrates. It is very high in iron and is, therefore, beneficial to growing bodies.

Black pepper seed tea
1 tsp Black pepper (freshly ground)
½ tsp Ginger
A squeeze of lemon
For one cup, boil until half the water is left (start with two cupfuls). A very warming and interesting flavour, useful for stomach upsets, especially for diarrhoea.

Fir tree teas
In general, these produce spicy, pungent flavours – quite delicious.

*Pine tea (*Pinus contorta latifolia *and other species)*
(Except *pinus massoniana* – unless birth control is desired.)
From the pine branches, gather several twigs with bushy needles at the tips. The younger growth of spring is best, but any time of year is fine. Strip the needles off.
75g Pine needles
12g Cinnamon
1 tsp Grated nutmeg
1 tsp Grated orange peel
Add to 1.8 litres of boiling water and infuse for 10 minutes. Add honey to taste. It has a delightful resinous flavour.
   This tea is lovely made over an open fire while camping and the use of the few pine needles cannot harm the tree.

*Spruce tea (*Picea sitchensis *and other species)*
As for the *Pine tea*, gather the spruce needles, preferably in the spring. Using a handful of needles per cup, it makes a very flavourable tea after infusing for 10 minutes. Either drink as it is or with additions.

*Larch tea (*Larix occidentalis *and other species)*
These leaves are deciduous and best picked in late spring and used fresh. Steep them for 5–10 minutes, and savour the resinous, pungent scented tea that will result! Add spices of your choice and/or grated lemon and orange peel to change the flavour slightly.

Douglas fir tea (Pseudotsuga menziesii)

Very rich in vitamin C, this is also a very tasty drink. Pour boiling water over a handful of young needles (although they are available all the year round) to make two cups of tea. Steep for 10 minutes or, for a stronger cup of tea, simmer for 20 minutes. Add spices and honey if desired.

Twig teas

My first introduction to twig teas was at college when I was offered a drink from a flask. Being a cold day and in need of warming up, I accepted without asking what the drink was. The drink was similar to coffee or root coffee and looked exactly like both. On enquiring, I was told that in haste my friend had picked some oak twigs, hazel twigs and birch twigs (it was mid-winter) and thrown them into a pot of boiling water to infuse for 10 minutes. Her reason for this was that she had used up all her teas in stock and needed something quickly. The taste was lovely and really tasted nicer without honey. Have a go and experiment yourselves!

Agar-agar tea

This is traditionally made from a selection of different seaweeds. Its major importance is its highly nutritive properties and large quantities of chlorophyll which oxygenates the body. It makes an excellent drink for those convalescing, and it helps prevent blood clotting. Beneficial for both diarrhoea and constipation.

Some famous names

Mate tea (Ilex paraguayensis)

This is a name familiar to most people and would be highly noticeable by its absence in this book. However, I did not include it in Chapter two or Chapter six because of its highly potent powers, due partly to its rich caffeine content.

Known also as 'Yerba mate' and 'Paraguay tea', it is a tea prepared from the leaves of the South American evergreen shrub, which is a close relative of our common holly. The leaves are oval and roughly six inches long, it also has tiny white flowers which, in turn, produce clusters of red berries growing close to the stem.

Mate plant

129

Mate was used as a caffeine beverage source by the native population of Latin America, centuries before coffee was introduced; it is still used.

The tea is prepared from the dried leaves, using one teaspoon per cup of boiling water. However, the old traditional, native procedure involves making a cold water infusion in a small bowl and inserting a hollow tube or straw through which to suck the tea. Nowadays, they put the leaves into a muslin bag and dangle this into a pot of boiling water by means of a piece of string. This is left for only two minutes and then removed – to be drunk by 'silver' straws.

The overall taste and smell is of toasted leaves and an infusion of not more than three minutes is advised – any longer produces a bitter flavour.

Rooibos, 'red-bush' or bushman tea

This plant comes from a South African tree and is drunk for its tonic properties all over the world. In Afrikaans, it is known as 'rooibos', which means 'red-bush'. The tea also possesses antihistamine properties. It is made by the normal infusion method.

Some more tasty additions

Before I go on to the section dealing with some of the fun teas which form just as much part of our lives as those in Chapter six, I would like to add some more ideas on embellishing herbal teas and recap on those already dealt with. This is because these embellishments are of particular importance in this next section.

Spruce essence

This lovely essence is obtained from our very familiar Christmas tree or Norway spruce (*picea abies*), and is indigenous to this country, although it had to be re-introduced in the sixteenth century.

For the essence, gather the young shoots (the outer sprigs and cones can also be used) in the spring, put them into a large pan (not aluminium) and cover with water. Bring to the boil and then simmer until the resinous flavour is extracted and the water is brown. Strain and return to the pan. Boil again until it is reduced by half, then bottle. Rich in natural preservatives, this essence will last years, but do label. It is lovely added to almost anything and is an excellent blood purifier.

Birch sap

The process of collection and usage of birch sap is many centuries old but, having done it once myself, I just felt too guilty to ever repeat the act. However, from an historical point of view I think it worth mentioning, and if you happen to have a large tree and pick exactly at the right moment, little harm can be done. Let me explain . . .

The tree should be large and tapped in early spring when the buds begin to swell (the sign that the sap is strongly rising) but *before* they open into leaves. Not only is the sap of superior quality, being clear, but this will not harm the tree – later on, the sap becomes thick and coloured, a sign that the sap rise is becoming slower and near the point when the tree cannot afford to lose its supply.

To tap the tree, bore a hole upwards at an angle of about thirty degrees (using a drill) to just beyond the bark where the sap rises. Insert a plastic

15th century method of collecting birch sap

tube that closely fits the hole and collect the sap in a well-secured bottle over several days. Most importantly, remember to plug the hole afterwards with a wooden plug and keep an eye on it in case of weeping. Birch sap is often used for wine when five to ten litres are needed, but, for herbal tea purposes, 300ml will go a long way as an essence.

Honey can be dissolved into this sap, ensuring self-preservation, although it has plenty of its own. This elixir of vitamins, minerals and nutrients can then be stored in dark, airtight bottles. Extremely pleasant tasting, it makes a lovely embellishment to most teas, having the added benefit of strengthening the kidneys and bladder. Helpful to rheumatism and arthritis.

Remember the list of essential oils from which you can choose, also the fruit juice concentrates. For any herbal tea, spices can be added at the last moment or crushed freshly, plus dried fruits such as elderberry, bilberry, raisins, etc. Although expensive nowadays, real vanilla pods have a lovely flavour. Break off a tiny piece and drop it into the cup or pot while infusing. Aniseed warms any tea and is excellent for breaking up excessive amounts of mucus.

Some more ideas for the botanical teapot

Ginger

Some people love ginger, while others simply cannot stand it, and I very often find there are no 'inbetweens' about this plant. Tastewise it is one of my great weaknesses and nothing is more delightful than grating fresh

131

ginger into the teapot on a cold winter's day, letting it infuse, adding a touch of, say, 'Wild Leatherwood Tree Honey' and sipping it slowly. You can literally feel its warmth slip between your bones and curl into every muscle and vein – sheer bliss.

For those who cannot find fresh ginger (try asking your greengrocer very persistently first, however), we have a very simple combination for you to try, using dried ingredients.

Ginger flake and cinnamon tea
Parts
10 Ginger (flakes)
1 Cinnamon
Simple, easy and delightful, the cinnamon adds just the right zing, reinforcing the ginger's activity. Wonderful for cramps, stomach pains, menstruation pains, chills, etc, and, drunk alongside a hot bath and a warm bed, it will cure anything!

Moving on to three ingredients and perhaps an opposite season.

Dragonflower tea (Lorna's tea)
Parts
5 Rosehips
5 Hibiscus (flower)
2 Rose petals
Try a dash of rose geranium oil – although I find it sweet enough without adding this and prefer it left alone. Drink on hot summer days from pretty bone china.

Summer tea
Parts
1 Lemon verbena (leaf)
1 Bergamot (leaf and flower)
1 Applemint (leaf)
2 Pineapple sage (leaf)
2 Borage (leaf)
Add grated orange peel and lime tree flavoured honey. Infuse as normal.

Tea of mints
Parts
2 Spearmint (leaf)
2 Peppermint (leaf)
1 Fresh catnip (leaf)
2 Nettle (leaf)
1 Drop of Brazilian peppermint
Infuse as normal.

Autumn berry tea
Parts
3 Bilberry
½ Rowan (berry)
2 Elderberry
½ Hawthorn (berry)
3 Juniper (berry)
1 Allspice
Infuse as normal, adding either rose oil or a dash of spruce essence – and, of course, honey.

The four seasons tea
While we are in the mood for seasonal teas, let me share a very popular flavoured one called 'The four seasons'. It has a strange quality about it and, although not an immediately appealing flavour, it grows on you – I know some people who drink nothing else. We call it 'The four seasons' because the herbs in it deal with all the problems of the different seasons: tonic, cleansing and energy-giving herbs for spring; vitamin, mineral and cooling herbs for summer; antiseptics and upper respiratory plants for autumn (for all colds, coughs, etc); and stimulating, warming and nutritive herbs for winter.
Equal parts of each
Sage (leaf)
Elderflower
Peppermint (leaf)
Ginger (flakes)
Sarsaparilla (root)
Thyme (leaf)
Alfalfa (leaf)
Buckwheat (leaf)
In spring one can add spruce essence or birch sap.
In autumn one can add hibiscus flowers (75g).
In summer one can add bergamot essential oil.
In winter one can add some sticks of cinnamon.

Jamaica spice tea (Kitty's tea)
The next tea I am going to discuss is a favourite with my step-daughter (and many of her school friends). She makes it with apple juice concentrate and drinks it hot in winter and cold in summer – delicious! Another person who has made this a great favourite of her own is my dear friend, Kitty Campion, and so sometimes I call this 'Kitty's tea' – while she herself christens it 'Jamaican sailor tea'. However, as many know it by its original name, that is what we will stick to here.

For many, including myself, it has proved wonderful for nausea of every description – travelling sickness and morning sickness, to name but two.
Parts
8 Ground pimento
8 Cinnamon sticks (broken)
½ Mace
½ Ginger (flakes)
½ Aniseed
½ Cardamom
½ Coriander
½ Liquorice
8 Lemon balm
1 Caraway
Infuse as normal.

Flower tea

This tea has great memories for me as it is the first tea I ever made and at the time I did not know much about herb blending. Quite by chance, I arrived at a very ancient blend of herbs, my nose and instinct leading me directly there. Elderflower and peppermint have been used for curing colds for centuries and, married with chamomile, for other similar purposes.

Delicately flavoured and producing a pretty colour in white china cups, it is particularly lovely in spring and summer. Made hot and drunk cold with fresh mint leaves, it is very cooling. Ideal also as a quieting, soothing tea drunk in the evening, any time of the year.
Parts
2 Lime treee (flower-crushed)
7 Elderflower
1½ Peppermint (leaf)
1 Hop (flower, crushed)
2 Chamomile (flower)
1 Blackthorn (flower, mildly purgative!)
Pinch of hibiscus flowers
2 Drops of Jaffa orange oil.
Add honey if desired, like lime tree flower blossom. Infuse as normal.

Lemon leaf tea
Parts
5 Lemon balm (leaf)
5 Lemon verbena (leaf)
2 Dill (seed)
1 Fennel (seed or leaf)
Oil of Lemon verbena
Zested or grated lemon peel

Infuse as normal. Lovely as an afternoon tea, soothing and settling after lunch, especially if there is a hint of indigestion. Full of flavour.

China light tea
The 'light' part of this name hopes to suggest its illuminating (spiritual) properties! And the China? That's a long story.
Parts
9 Lavender (flower)
5 Rosemary (leaf)
5 Peppermint (leaf)
1 Lime tree (flower)
½ Hop (flower)
2 Meadowsweet (flower and leaf)
Infuse as normal, adding lime tree flowers or Chinese poppy honey.

Fruity spice tea
This tea is also lovely put into muslin squares and used for mulling with red wine on a very cold winter's day.
Equal parts of each
Cloves (whole)
Cinnamon (broken sticks)
Ginger (flakes)
Mace (whole)
½ part Cumin
Sloes (whole, ripe)
Rosehips (chopped)
Hibiscus flowers
Nutmeg, ground (not during pregnancy)
Elderberry (whole)
Infuse as normal, using buckwheat honey to flavour further. If mulling the mixture, then a dash of cinnamon oil is nice, especially as some of the flavours are simmered off in preparation.

Red tea
Parts
5 Bushman's tea (red-bush, or rooibos)
2 Hibiscus (flower)
1 Rosehips
1 Rose petals
½ Elderberry
1 Sloes (blackthorn fruits – slightly binding)
Creating a lovely red-coloured tea, this is fragrant, tasty and a good tonic. Infuse as normal, adding red clover honey.

135

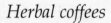

Herbal coffees

I discussed the character and making of herbal coffees in Chapter four, with their main distinction from teas being that they are usually made from roasted roots, seeds, nuts, etc. I promised some recipes in Chapter four – so here they are. But before we make the change to herbal coffees, let me suggest a lovely combination while switching over to herbal coffees which involves real coffee and herbs; a gentle substitution.

Dr Singha's coffee
1 Cup real bean coffee
2 Cardamom (white for females and black for males)
A few fennel leaves (fresh, if possible)
Sweeten with honey if desired.

Dandelion coffee
Equal parts
Dandelion (roasted)
Chocolate
The next is an old recipe and one not to be encouraged too often! But try substituting with carob, adding lots of honey to counteract the slightly bitter taste.
Parts
5 Dandelion
1 Chicory
Infuse both recipes as normal.

The proportion of chicory to dandelion should always be less as it has a strong flavour, much more so than coffee! This combination was frequently used in the war as a substitute. Chicory grows wild all over Britain, particularly in the southern regions, enjoying most soils and showing off its wonderful bright blue compositae flowers. As a perennial, it can be used as a very useful vegetable.

Another partner to dandelion can be the acorn. In Germany, acorn coffee was the national beverage during the rationing of the First World War. While having beneficial antiseptic and digestive properties, it also tastes not unlike coffee. A tea can also be made out of the oak leaves.
125g Dandelion
75g Acorns (roast in a moderate oven until dark brown and dry, then grind)
Infuse as above.

Pod and seed coffee
Goosegrass, as a distant relative to the coffee plant, produces many seeds from its white, star-like flowers. Sometimes known as cleavers (*galim*

aparaine), it sticks to anything it touches and many a child has taken delight in throwing it at the unsuspecting. The juice of the leaf, like chickweed, is excellent for skin problems and is also an effective diuretic – while the whole herb is good for insomnia. So this has to be rated as a calming, water reducing tea, especially as it is a well-known and time-old diuretic.

In equal parts

Broom pods

Goosegrass seeds

Dry the goosegrass seeds, roast for a few minutes in a hot oven, then grind and prepare like coffee. Collect the broom pods but remove the seeds – a laborious task! Roast the pods in a hot oven, being careful not to burn them, then grind or pound with a mortar.

This herb coffee is well worth the effort; it really has a delightful and unique flavour.

Beech nut coffee

Beech nuts have been used as a nutritious farm fodder (like acorns) for centuries. In America, their use as a coffee substitute was common, along with using the ground oil and meal from the nut as beech nut butter.

The nuts should be peeled, then roasted in a hot oven until dry and brittle. Infuse like the other coffees, adding spices and honey to taste.

Juniper roast coffee

Perhaps a rather unsuspecting ingredient but, roasted and combined with nutmeg or cinnamon (and a little honey), the taste is delicious.

Parts

7 Roast juniper berries (good for the urinary tract; antiseptic)

½ Broken cinnamon sticks

½ Liquorice (rhizome)

Roast all ingredients in a slow oven until dark brown, then grind finely. Using one tablespoon to a cup of boiling water, allow to steep for a short while. Delicious!

Note: Be careful not to overuse this drink as juniper is a strong diuretic and can overwork the kidneys with prolonged use.

Coffee substitute

A lovely coffee formula, this really does taste surprisingly like coffee. I have been caught out with this recipe in the past!

Parts

5 Dandelion (root)

2 Burdock

1 Liquorice (root)

½ Cinnamon (bark)

2 Acorns
1 Chicory
1 Oak (bark)
½ Orris (root)

Either roast these ingredients singly to their maximum point, or roast altogether. Leave to cool, then grind, using one tablespoon per 475ml boiling water. Alter the strength to taste.

Delicious with or without honey, although the addition of the liquorice adds a natural and subtle sweetness to offset some of the bitter ingredients.

Root roast coffee
Equal parts of each
Sarsaparilla
Dandelion
Burdock
Sassafras
Comfrey root
Marshmallow root
Liquorice

Make as for the previous coffee, adding a dash of bergamot orange oil, after grinding, to add a hint of flavour.

A final note . . .
Loving cup tea

I felt that it would be rather nice to end this book on an embracing, loving note, and so I have chosen a healing infusion of herbs – in all senses of the word! The herbs are also attractive and romantic, and ones that are stimulative to passions, as well as soothing to more negative emotions. Try it and see!

Parts
2 Violets (rich in vitamins A and C)
1 Rosemary (flower and leaf)
5 Mate
5 Elderflower
1 Rose petals
1 Marigold (flower)
1 Lime tree (flowers and leaves)
1 Blackthorn (leaf) (similar in taste to China tea)

Use both black and white cardamom for Yang and Yin effect.

Infuse as normal, adding a touch of rose geranium oil, apple blossom or bluebell honey.

Glossary

Alterative Alterative herbs are usually used to combat toxicity in the body. They gradually and favourably alter the condition of the body.

Analgesic A substance that produces insensibility to pain without loss of consciousness.

Antibiotic A substance that inhibits the growth of, or destroys, bacteria, viruses and amoebae. Many antibiotics have a direct germ-killing effect but most act to stimulate the body's own immune response.

Antihistamine Antihistamine herbs act against a histamine. A histamine is a substance formed in damaged human tissue but can be the poison in a nettle and the sting of an insect.

Antispasmodic Antispasmodic herbs relieve nervous irritability and reduce excessive involuntary muscle contraction or spasm.

Astringent A substance that causes contraction, shrinkage or firming of living tissue.

Carminative Carminative herbs reduce flatulence and colic.

Demulcent A smooth and soothing substance.

Deobstruent Deobstruent herbs dissolve bodily accumulations and remove them from the body by rendering them fluid and increasing perspiration.

Diaphoretic Diaphoretic herbs promote perspiration.

Diuretic Diuretic herbs increase the volume and frequency of urination.

Emesis Vomiting.

Expectorant A substance that promotes the expulsion of fluid from the lungs and air passage.

Laxative A substance that promotes bowel movement.

Morbid accumulation The build up of harmful substances (usually highly toxic) within the body.

Narcotic A substance that produces sleep and relieves pain. In large doses it can cause poisoning with coma or convulsions.

Nutritive Nutritive herbs provide substantial amounts of balanced minerals and vitamins in an easily assimilable form.

Purgative A strong laxative that increases peristalsis.

Sedative Sedative herbs quicken the nervous system. They are usually only used short term in crises.

Stimulant Stimulant herbs increase the energy and warmth of the body.

Index

Jill Davies

Jill Davies (with her partner) runs her own commercial walled herb garden, the home of their original herb tea blends which are sold all over the world. She trained at the Royal Horticultural Society Gardens, Wisley and the Royal Botanic Gardens, Kew. She also qualified as a Master Herbalist at the School of Natural Healing in Utah, U.S.A. and she is now the co-director of the School's U.K. facility. Jill Davies is a member of the British Herbal Medicine Association. She practised herbal medicine and lectures extra murally at Cambridge University. She lives with her family in Suffolk.

Notes

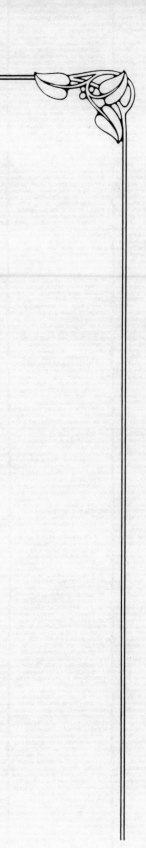

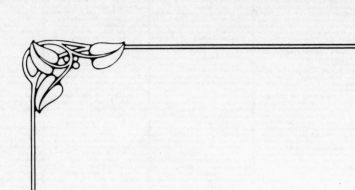

Notes

Notes